CONTENTS

PAIRING
WINE
AND
FOOD

Linda Johnson-Bell

BURFORD BOOKS

DEDICATION

For Michael and Benjamin

Printed in the United States of America

10 9 8 7 6 5 4 3

Library of Congress Cataloging-in-Publication Data
Johnson-Bell, Linda.
    Pairing wine and food / Linda Johnson-Bell.
        p.   cm.
    Includes bibliographical references.
    ISBN 1-58080-037-8 (pb)
    1. Food.   2. Wine and wine making.   I. Title.
TX353.J63   1999
641.2'2—dc21   99-32432
                                              CIP

PAIRING
WINE
AND
FOOD

INTRODUCTION

I very immodestly consider myself a wine expert, and a purist at that. At first, I never paid very much attention to food. It was simply what came with my wine. I cringed when waiters in restaurants brought the food menu first, treating the wine selection as an afterthought. Anyone who didn't consider wine as first and foremost, and who didn't insist that the food bow to the superior power of the grape, was a heathen, in my book. But no more. I no longer ridicule food writers or those attention-hungry chefs who become pop stars (well, not as much as I used to). For I have married the enemy: a "foodie."

Do not get me wrong, I am not a stranger to good food. I came from one of those rare American households where fast food and cola drinks were *verboten*, where dinner was a formal ritual, and where every meal was fresh and original. In addition, for more than ten years, I wallowed in gastronomic excess while living in France, scouring the daily markets for the freshest produce, making hundreds of pots of homemade *confiture,* and attending almost every Michelin-star restaurant opening. I even prepared and ate things that still wriggle in your dish when served. I *did* the French thing—wholly and completely. But I did it from a wine drinker's perspective. With hindsight, however, I realize that a love of food was slowly infusing into my subconscious, without my knowledge or consent.

My foodie owns a wonderful restaurant in London's Portobello Road. I found myself surrounded. I had no choice but to convert. Now, all day long, magnificent odors waft about me. I find myself engrossed in conversation with the chefs over how long squid should be marinated for the ceviche, which spices would best liven up the vegetarian dishes, and which wines would best complement the new menus.

Suddenly, I was speaking another language. Force-fed a diet of freshly picked wild raspberries, duck egg omelettes, home-grown salads filled with nasturtium leaves, rose petals, chives, rocket, three different varieties of mint, lavender, and rosemary. Not to mention fresh oysters with horseradish and lime, sashimi of salmon with wasabi and fresh ginger, sweet potato with peanut and coriander pesto, roast pork with crackling, and banoffee pie. My foodie had introduced me to the other side of the equation—my taste buds couldn't keep up. It worked. I was seduced. He didn't get me drunk, he just got me properly fed—something I was told would never happen to me in England!

It is fun. It is interesting. And, suddenly, it all makes sense. We can only really know and understand wine and the taste of it if we know and understand the same about food. They are mated for life.

The tradition of enjoying food and wine together has become so much a part of our daily routine that it is practically involuntary: food on table, wine in glass. What could be more natural? We whip up a creamy fettuccine Alfredo, deftly uncork a bottle of crisp Chianti, throw on some Pavarotti and light some candles and *voilà!* We've usually mastered this scenario (and what follows!) by the time we leave college. But why does this classic combination work so well? How did we know that the fresh Parmesan and nutmeg, the dominant flavors in the pasta, would go so nicely with the Sangiovese grape that dominates the wine? We are all familiar with the golden rules of wine service, passed to us through years of Sunday lunches with the family or gleaned from the jacket flaps of recipe books. Rules such as a "White meat takes white wine; red meat, red wine," and "White wine before red," and so on. But did you ever stop to think why? Why do food and wine taste the way they do and why are these tastes so varied?

With today's plethora of international foods and wines available, the choices can become overwhelming. If you are confused as to how to match wine with food, put away your beer and despair no more. It is easier than you think. For, despite the apparent complexity of matches, you have been deceived. Most information available to us takes a generic and simplistic approach: Lamb goes well with red wine, for example. Or they go to the other extreme and are overly specific: Icelandic lamb of a specific age with a curry and coconut milk sauce with a dash of coriander and parsley goes well with "So-and-so's wine of one or two particular vintages of the last decade, unattainable in the States, made of an obscure grape variety, served at fifty-nine degrees Fahrenheit."

Actually, it is not the lamb you should be worrying about at all. Here is the secret: Marry the dominant flavor of the dish (usually found in the sauce) to the dominant grape variety of the wine. This is the crux of the situation. Basic ingredient meets basic ingredient (worry about texture and weight later). An Indian lamb curry dish may be better with a spicy, acidic white such as a Gewürztraminer, whereas a classic lamb roast in gravy with roast potatoes and mint sauce would prefer a rich Pomerol or New World Cabernet Sauvignon. (Note that Cabernet Sauvignon is the dominant grape variety used in the Cabernet Sauvignon, Cabernet Franc, and Merlot Bordeaux blend in Pomerol.)

But we can make things even easier. It is not just about Indian food going best with spicy whites and Chinese with tannic reds—but about the sweet, sour, salty, or spicy flavor of the food going with the sweetness, acidity, bitterness, or astringency of the wine. Nowhere does there exist a comprehensive compilation of dishes with an explanation of *why* things taste the way they taste, and therefore match or don't match. This guide will provide that information.

In addition to listing specific dishes, you will also be given an explanation from the specific to the general. Illogical, you might say, but working first with specific flavors, then their groups, then the dishes, does make sense.

Furthermore, you will discover the reasons why some pairings work and others don't, how the classic marriages developed, how to vary taste themes without disastrous results, and the industry's secrets and remedies when dealing with wine's sworn enemies.

It is interesting to note that all this used to be very easy—that is, if you lived in Rome or Peking or Delhi. If you were a local inhabitant of any of these places—so recognizable as the origins of our regular take-out places—you wouldn't have to think twice about your accompanying brew. Having to worry about what goes with what is a relatively modern dilemma.

Every country or region that is known for a particular specialty produces a wine or other alcoholic beverage intended to strike the perfect
accord with its food. Usually, it is also a home-grown product created from
pretty much the same ingredients that are in the food. The Romans drink
Frascati Superiore Secco with their *spaghetti alla carbonara,* the Swiss enjoy
Chasselas with their cheese fondue, the North Africans choose fig alcohol
and mint tea with their couscous, the Russians serve vodka with their
borscht, and the Scandinavians appreciate aquavit with their gravlax.

These rich food and drink pairings are often regional. Nowhere is this
clearer than in Italy or France. In France, one drinks Riesling with *choucroute
garnie à l'alsacienne,* Sancerre with Chavignol cheese, and Sauternes with foie
gras. None of this has come about by accident, but by design—nature's
design. Wine is simply made from grapes, and grapes are fruit, which are
grown just like any other fruit or crop. Fruit born of the same soil, in the
same climate, and of the same environment, very naturally make perfect bed-
fellows.

This gets a little more difficult in countries that have brought everything with them, so to speak! The United States is a perfect example.
Theoretically, the staples of the Native American—corn, potatoes, beans,
squash, pumpkin, tomatoes, and fried bread—were married to whatever they
drank locally: cactus juice, whiskey given to them by the cavalry? The
Mexicans used beans, chiles, and corn, adapted to their tastes, and soothed
their burning tongues with tequila, while the European settlers of the West
relied heavily on sourdough bread and pinto beans. Until, that is, they moved
in completely and imposed their preferences from home, with hybrids such
as clam chowder and pumpkin pie being the results. American cuisine today
is a complete fusion of local and regional crops mixed with the recipes and
foodstuffs imported and planted by the immigrants. Hence you'll find Dutch
dishes in Pennsylvania, French dishes in Louisiana, and, of course, Italian,
Jewish, Polish, German, and more in New York, where many of the original
immigrants first arrived.

Whereas food may vary from region to region in the U.S., the bulk of
the wine production is limited to one or two states and is modeled after the
European noble grape styles rather than to suit or complement a regional
style. It is also marginal in terms of quantities produced and consumed in
proportion to the corresponding influx of ethnic food influences. It was easier to grow wheat and make pasta like Mama used to make, but far more
difficult to transport and plant the vines. Thus, America's drinking heritage
relied mainly on spirits. Kentucky is a perfect example. It is a mini culture
revolving around bourbon whiskey. Their entire social season is fueled, quite

literally, by the famous and enormously refreshing mint julep. But it gets better! There are bourbon candy balls, bourbon cake, bourbon jelly, and, of course, the main dish, burgoo.

Drought, depression, world wars, and prohibition at one point crippled America's wine industry. So although the culinary aspect is rich and well developed, the task of wine pairing is a problem for most Americans. Our wine heritage needs to catch up with our culinary evolution. We just have not had the opportunity to do with wines what we have done with food. There are few indigenous grape varieties that grew up with complementary regional flavor groups. We are obliged to choose from the imported European grape varieties. And with everyone planting pretty much the same ones, our choice can become comparatively limited.

What is happening is that we are, in a way, reinventing the wheel. We are having to analyze and work at something that has always been second nature to our European forebears. Today we are so concerned about food and wine pairings that we have even coined the term *food wines* to denote wines that are easily matched to foods. This is both a good and a bad thing. It is true that in an effort to persuade consumers to consider wine an everyday beverage, essential to a healthy diet, it has to be associated with food. Heavy marketing of wine as an accompaniment to food was the only direction to take, using the European culture as a model. Unfortunately it has almost gone too far, and consumers now don't expect anything more from a wine than that it costs less than eight dollars and that it goes with an entire meal. Heaven forbid it overshadows the Thai sauce on the shrimp.

We are overlooking the importance of a wine's personality. Some wine producers have gone as far as to deliberately to make easy, light, noncommittal wines for this reason: They are marketable and consumer friendly and are getting the job done. But these are probably not wines you would always want on your table. Yes, if you are feeling lazy, it is easy to grab a noncommittal companion who will agree with everything you say. But isn't it far more interesting and agreeable to have companions with personalities and opinions of their own?

This lack of originality may have come about because although ethnic foods have been successfully imported, the corresponding beverages have not, so for many countries, the wine/food equation has been lost.

Luckily, more and more regional wines from Europe are becoming accessible. We have not only more wines from new countries being imported, but a more varied selection from countries we already know. For example, the French imports are no longer restricted to Burgundy and Bordeaux but now include all their lovely satellite regions.

The problem with some of the typical local wines we only see while on vacation in Europe is that they are produced in such small quantities that there is not enough to export. For example, Hungary's goulash has been duplicated, copied, and Westernized for ages, whereas their wines, such as Tokàji or Kékfrankos, are relatively unknown. Thus we have little choice but to drink Burgundy with our goulash, which might very well work, but was not what the plains cowboys in Hungary enjoyed. (Actually, I doubt that they sat around the campfire commenting on the steely mineral backbone of a Tokàji, but you know what I mean!)

Some would argue that the reason these wines never left home is that they are undrinkable or subject to low technical and even lower hygiene standards. This is hardly a problem anymore (though I personally like a little dirt in my wine). But I would argue that if they had the international recognition needed to provide the funds and regenerate the industry, then these problems would be corrected and a regional style could be preserved, within traditional parameters yet on a larger scale. And this is what is happening. Countries like Portugal, Romania, and Hungary are receiving investment and are refusing to enter the international market by riding on the fame and reputation of the ubiquitous, well-known European grape varieties. They argue that if they are obliged to remarket their wine's reputation, why not use that as an opportunity to educate wine drinkers and to market their own grape varieties and wine styles?

This is a brave step, especially in a market where the simple word *Chardonnay* on a bottle label can triple profits. But the market, as well as the consumer, is changing. The first step was to get us drinking wines from countries we could not even point to on a map. The next is to introduce us to grape varieties and styles that, while traditional in their own right, are presented as "new and different" to the international consumer. Better yet, it is time for our domestic wine producers to start looking at grape varieties other than the classic European noble models. The U.S. has climates to suit almost all of them.

So with more food and wine choices available than ever before, where do you begin? If you understand the workings of flavor groups, then you will easily master the game of food and wine matches. This guide will put you in control of your palate and your imagination. Part 1 explains what gives wine its taste, and I go much farther than simply the grape variety—I go to its true origins and examine everything about its composition. In part 2, I do the same with food, thus making very clear the analogous relationship of food and wine. In part 3, the extensive cross-references should cover every imaginable match you could conceive. If you find any oversights or omissions, please do not hesitate to let me know!

When you understand why food and wine taste as they do, you can understand why and how the classic rules have developed, which then gives you the freedom and confidence to break or adapt them in clever and personal ways. Take sweet white wines, for example. The English call them "dessert" wines—how shortsighted! A good sweet white can be served alone as an aperitif, with a first course of foie gras or quiche, with a main course of roast pork stuffed with prunes or apricots, with a fruit salad or a green salad made with walnuts, and is sublime with blue cheese, Roquefort, mild and strong goat's cheeses (but not the sweet, creamy kind), and Epoisses or Beaufort cheeses. And all of this before you even get to dessert! Another surprise is Champagne. We forget that Champagne is a wine that can take a meal from beginning to end—nothing beats ending a meal with a light and digestible Champagne.

So, break all the rules. The essential is that both personalities are respected and complemented, and not dominated. Just like the most timid and introverted individuals can become enlivened when in the presence of an outgoing companion, a good food match can reveal the many complexities of a wine. It is not about compensating each other's deficiencies, but rather underlining and bringing forward their respective qualities. A wine, no matter how good, will not be able to render a boring, bland dish more interesting. Equally so, an unbalanced or dull wine will not have its faults masked by a spicy, spectacular dish. If a wine has brought forward an aspect of the food and the food has reinforced an element of the wine, then a successful match has been made. And as with all things in life, this is easily achieved with mutual respect, coupled with inquisitiveness; with patience, peppered with a dash of ambition; with passion, lightly tempered with moderation; and with experience gained through much practice!

Let pleasure be your guide.

—LINDA JOHNSON-BELL
(lindawines@hotmail.com,
www.lindajohnsonbell.com)

PART I

THE
TASTE
OF
WINE

When I first started learning about wine, I was twenty years old and studying in Paris. The French family with which I was living was a noble old family that, like many others, had little more than their titles and the crumbled remains of a château as reminders of their glorious past. My baroness had a heart of gold. Her dear husband, although I adored him for it, was a clever, quite frugal conniver who had turned cheating the system into his livelihood. (This is a very French thing, by the way.) One evening, early in the year, they organized a dinner party for all the family to view the new American arrival. For this auspicious occasion, they brought out a bottle of wine that, I was proudly told, was produced by one of their family members in Bordeaux. As prior gustatory forays at my California girls' school had only introduced me to the delights of *California Coolers* and strawberry daiquiris, I was very intimidated and was trying desperately to keep my virgin palate in the closet.

The wine was presented with what I thought then was great style and tradition. With hindsight, I can assure you that it was pure blundering pomp. I tasted it. They all looked at me. What was I supposed to say? That it tasted good? Did it? How was I supposed to know? I had nothing with which to compare it. Because I did appreciate that it had a little more "umph" than my last gallon of Gallo Burgundy, I said so—but not in so many words, of course. The rest of the family was served the wine and very soon we had duly drained the last drop from the bottle. Yet it sat there, empty, until one of the cousins pointed out that we were in need of more refreshment. Baron de Plouc scowled at the cousin, picked up the bottle, and took it back to the kitchen. He reappeared a few minutes later with a fresh bottle, this time served without any of the previous hullabaloo. I noticed that he had uncorked it in the kitchen. Glasses were happily refilled and we drank on.

But wait a minute. Something was definitely very strange. This glass of wine tasted distinctly unlike our first glass. I discreetly looked at the bottle that was still proudly on display in the middle of the table and confirmed that, yes indeed, it was the same wine as the first. Actually, it was even the same bottle as the first! It had the same little water stain on top of the *m* in *mis en bouteille*. Being an inexperienced young Yank, I said nothing and kept drinking, deciding that there must be more to this wine game than I thought. I looked around the room and no one else seemed even to bat a taste bud. This went on all evening; the bottle kept disappearing and coming back to the table full.

The party became quite gay. Baron de Plouc now only needed a cursory glance from the cousin before performing his hostly duties. After five more bottles of decidedly inferior red brew had been served, I chose to investigate. I followed Baron de Plouc into the kitchen on the pretext that I was going to help clean up. And what did I spy? Baron bending over the family's precious heritage, pouring the contents of a two-liter container of Felix Potin's twelve-franc-a-liter, generic red wine through the funnel I'd seen him use to fill up the Renault Cinq last week. He saw me and my aghast expression, and shot me a conspiratorial smile accompanied by a hissing *Dites-rien, d'accord?* I agreed, and morosely went back out to join the other guests.

Voilà. One of my very first interludes with French wine. Believe it or not, that very same bottle appeared on the table every time we had important guests for dinner—and I never said a word.

LEARNING ABOUT WINE

I continued my wine education on my own by soaking off and saving the bottle labels of every wine I tasted, even bothering wine waiters in restaurants. I would glue the labels into my wine notebook and write down the date, the place, the meal, and my companions, and then note my impressions. At the beginning, I could usually only muster an "I like this" or " I do not like this." Not a very encouraging start but it did actually work because, before too long, I could look at all the wines I did like and find their common denominator, thereby determining my first preferences. Eventually, I was able to detect differences between the wines and then was able to put names to these tastes.

You may be asking, Why go to all this bother? Today, wine labels are increasingly informative, telling you what sort of foods the wine will match, and often even including information on the region's climate or soils. But not having to rely on commercial copy scripted by the wineries' PR team, and learning the ground rules about what goes into the taste of wine— which you will learn from this section of the book—will help you to assess and taste wines, better understanding your preferences and better matching your food and wine. The first lesson you learn when tasting wines is what you like and do not like. This is half the battle. The other half is learning why you like them or do not like them. If you can then find the common denominators—grape variety, wine style, regional preference, and so on— you have come a long way and the rewards will be many!

WHAT IS TASTE?

So what is taste? We tend to take our sense of taste for granted. Do you realize that—just as with our senses of hearing, sight, and touch—we constantly taste things even when we are not eating? For the senses of smell and taste are so closely linked that we always taste what we smell and vice versa. The two work in conjunction with one another. Furthermore, our sense of sight also aids our sense of taste. Our whole sensorial repertoire tells us what a piece of burnt toast is going to taste like even before we put it into our mouth.

In the same way that different people have different strengths of eyesight or hearing, so people are born with different abilities in the areas of taste and smell, which are further influenced by our cultural and sensorial pasts. So each individual has uniquely tuned physiological mechanisms that

release or stimulate a reaction and therefore a personal minimum and maximum threshold of taste and smell perception. Like the other senses, smell
and taste serve as a source of information for our brains. Our sensorial logic
then discriminates and identifies those different sensations.

When we taste something, we experience a sensation in special parts
of the mouth: the taste buds. These are dispersed throughout the mouth, and
some have specific sensors: Sourness is recognized with the tip of the
tongue; sweetness with the flat of the tongue; bitterness under the tongue;
tartness on the inner surface of the cheeks.

We have tried endlessly to create a finite classification of flavors, but
as each individual will interpret a substance differently, a standard of measurement can only be vague and subjective. However, we do know that we
can classify the larger taste groups of sweetness, acidity, saltiness, sourness,
and bitterness. But even with these groups, the boundaries are far from pre-
cise. It is difficult to establish a clear demarcation between one type and
another, because the taste of individual foods or wines comes, in fact, from
a combination of these basic flavors. Also, our ability to perceive the flavors
themselves is influenced by other factors such as temperature and flavor
combinations.

HOW A GOOD UPBRINGING ENSURES GOOD TASTE

What influences a wine's taste? First of all, what is wine? Wine is simply the
result of the partial or entire alcoholic fermentation of fresh grapes or the
juice of fresh grapes. It tastes like the things it contains, therefore the pre-
dominant flavors of wine come from the skin, or just beneath the skin, of
the grapes used to make it.

In the simplest terms, wine is composed of: water (between 75 and 90
percent), alcohols, acids, polyphenols (or coloring agents), sugars (fructose
and glucose), carbon dioxide, and aromatic components (chemicals). In addition to these, there are also all the components of wine that we cannot see,
smell, or taste, such as vitamins, proteins, amino acids, and so on. Each of
these plays an important role in the taste of a wine.

Like human beings, a wine's taste is going to depend a great deal on
both its origins and its upbringing. In fact, the French use this very word—
élevage or "upbringing"—when describing a wine's early life.

The taste of a wine is therefore the result of the combination of many
factors, starting with the unique characteristics of the grape variety, or varieties, used to make it. The next factors are how the vines were planted, grown,

pruned, and treated; the soil and subsoil; the general climate of the vineyard's region; and sometimes even the climate of the surrounding areas. Were the vines grown on a fertile valley floor or clinging to a steep slope? Did they have to fight for food or were they overfertilized and overwatered? Did they get too much sunshine or just what they needed? Were they allowed to produce all the fruit they wanted (the French call this *"pissing"* the vines) or were they pruned and obliged to produce fewer but better-quality grapes? The vintage year will also affect the taste of a wine, as the weather and growing conditions are never the same from one year to the next.

The vinification method, how the wine was treated before being bottled, and how long it has been left to mature in the bottle all add to its unique flavor combination. Will it be a flash-in-the-pan sort of wine or will it mature nicely and develop even more character as it grows old? All in all, has it been disciplined or spoiled rotten? A spoiled vine, like a spoiled child, will produce a lazy, brash, and superficial wine. A wine with character will behave more subtly and will reveal its strength and personality as you get to know it.

WHAT DOES WINE TASTE LIKE?

The taste elements of both wine and food are the same: sweetness, acidity, bitterness, and astringency.

The sweetness in the taste of wine comes from the fructose and glucose, types of sugar, in the grape and from the alcohol produced during the fermentation. The alcohol is not sweet in itself, it just underlines those components that are, and helps counteract the acidity and tannins, making the wine appear sweeter.

The acidity comes from the tartaric and malic acids in the grapes. Malic acid is green tasting and can make wine very bitter, which is why the fermentation processes chosen by the winemaker are so important in achieving a balance. They will affect the malic acid levels in the wine.

Bitterness and astringency come from the tannins in the grapes. There are very few tannins in white wines, so most discussion of tannins is reserved for the reds.

The Taste of Acidity

The sour-tasting substances in wine are the acids: Tartaric, malic, and citric are in the grape; succinic, lactic, and acetic result from fermentation. The total acidity of a wine depends upon whether the growing season was too cold—in which case the grapes are too acidic and underripe—or too hot—in which case the grapes become overripe and lack acids. White wines generally have more acidity than reds. It is the amount of acid that is important: Too little and the wine is bland and flabby, too much and it is vinegary. The right amount of acid, in balance with the wine's other components, makes the wine look and taste crisp, clean, and lively, as well as ensuring longevity.

Tartaric acid is unique to grapes and to wine and represents one-quarter to one-third of the total acid composition of wine. It is the strongest acid and it strongly influences the pH of a wine. The pH measures the concentration of hydrogen ions, which for wine means its dryness. The lower the pH, the safer the wine is from diseases and from oxidation, and therefore the greater its aging potential. The tartaric acid content decreases as the grape ripens, then varies depending upon the harvest weather conditions.

Malic acid is found in every part of the grapevine. It is the most fragile of the acids, which allows for its easy transformation into lactic acids (called malolactic fermentation), which diminishes considerably the overall acidity of a wine. The hotter the year's weather, the faster the acid decreases during the ripening process, which is why there is more of it when the weather has been cooler. All red wines are allowed to go through a complete malolactic fermentation. White wines can either go without, go partially through, or go entirely through this second fermentation. It depends upon the juice's initial acid and sugar levels and the style of wine desired. If a winemaker wants a crisp and green white wine, then the malolactic fermentation is halted or not even allowed to begin. For a buttery, smooth white, the malolactic fermentation is permitted for longer or until its completion.

Acids give a wine its shine or brilliance—especially the tartaric acids, which renew the wine's color. It is the presence of malic acid that often gives a wine an apple smell, and in the mouth we can sense the amount of acids by the irritation of our gums and the inside of the mouth.

The Taste of Tannins: Bitterness and Astringency

The most important of the three types of polyphenols, or coloring agents, tannins give a wine texture rather than taste. Tannins that are condensed are present in the grape, and those that are exogene are procured from the wood during barrel aging. In the stalks, skins, and pips there are tannins that are released during fermentation and pressing, giving the wine its specific character and contributing to its aging capacity. Storing, or aging, the wine in oak introduces additional tannins (the newer the oak, the more tannins), which are transferred from the wood's fibers. These are more common in red wine than in white. Tannins obtained from the oak barrels can improve a wine's aging potential, complement its texture, and fill it out, but only if the wine itself has a solid backbone of acids, fruit extracts, and condensed tannins. Oak aging cannot replace the raw materials that are lacking in the first place.

The wine's red color fades as the anthocyanins, another tannin, diminish with age. The more mature a wine, the more yellow or brown the disk, or surface, becomes. The combination of these coloring agents can give the wine a sour taste and a drying sensation in the mouth. This is called astringency. Different tannins from different-aged wines and wines from various regions will have distinct sorts of astringency. For example, young Bordeaux will have tough, astringent tannins, while old Bordeaux will have velvet-soft tannins. The more tannin is present in a wine's youth, the more it makes the sides of your mouth pucker, and the longer it will take to mature. Don't buy a recent-vintage Bordeaux Premier Cru and expect it to go down like velvet; it is meant to age and mature in the bottle. This is why bottle aging is so important, as we will see later.

The Taste of Sweetness

There are three major sweet-tasting substances in wine: the sugars and polyalcohols, both originating in the grape, and alcohols from fermentation.

Each style of wine has a different level of sugar, depending upon the grapes' maturation when harvested. Sweet wines contain several dozen grams of sugar per liter, while a dry white wine normally contains less than two grams per liter. The sugars, along with the alcohols, give the wine body and are visible because of the "legs" formed on the side of the glass. The sugars don't really have any odor but could eventually contribute to the overall expression of the wine. And it is the sugar that gives the wine its sweet taste, its fatness, and its unctuousness.

Alcohol is an important element in wine—it gives it great-looking legs. It is produced during fermentation when enzymes created by the yeasts change the sugar of the grape juice into alcohol, carbon dioxide, and heat. It is the proportion of alcohol to glycerin that determines the limpidity, or the body, of a wine, which we observe as legs or tears. More alcohol and the wine is thinner, thus the legs run down the side of the glass more quickly. The more glycerin is present, the thicker the wine will be, and thus the more slowly the legs will drip down the side of the glass. It is also primarily the amount of ethyl alcohol that will determine the sweetness of the wine.

The Taste of Bubbles

Carbon dioxide is the principal product, along with ethyl alcohol, of the alcoholic fermentation. It is present in both still wines and effervescent wines. If the wine is effervescent, carbon dioxide manifests itself as bubbles.

Like tannin, bubbles do not have an odor or taste as such, but the bubbles help release the wine's perfumes and definitely alter its texture. If anything, you can detect an acidic taste edge while it pricks and tickles the tongue.

FOR A FRAGRANT SMELL

Aromatic components (chemical substances) exist in minuscule quantities in wine and are issued from various chemical groups: alcohols, acids, ethers, and so on. For example, the presence of ethyl acetate might smell like vinegar, phenylethyl acetate like rose, ethyl caproate like soap, menthol like mint, and vanillin like vanilla.

What is important to note is that these are all visual, olfactive, and gustative results born of the wine itself, its contents. In addition to these, there are other man-made manipulations, such as adding fabricated yeasts to the grape juice to jump-start fermentation (rather than encouraging the indigenous yeasts to form), and other measures that are taken to rectify nature's flaws of low sugars and high acidity, which also alter the smell and taste of wine. I'll discuss these later.

 ## THE SMELLS OF WINE

The following is an exhaustive list of the various smells and aromas a wine can have. A wine's smell can tell you a lot about how it was made, where it is from, how old it is, and whether or not it is of good quality. Identifying a wine's smell also develops your taste memory, which is indispensable when trying to establish what kind of wine you prefer and when matching food and wine. Do not forget that smell and taste remain subjective senses; not everybody will taste the same odor, or will identify it as the same thing. Also remember that despite the general rules and guidelines of winemaking, there are always exceptions.

FAMILY OF SMELLS	EXAMPLES	COMMENTS
Floral	Acacia Carnation Hawthorn or mayapple Honeysuckle Narcissus Vine Wildflowers	These are considered to be good odors and are found in young, dry white wines and sparkling wines.

FAMILY OF SMELLS	EXAMPLES	COMMENTS
	Broom Jasmine Lime blossom Rose Violet	These are more present and heavy and are found in serious white wines that will age, and in some red wines. Look for rose in a Gewürztraminer or Muscat.
	Geranium	A very strong presence of this flower usually indicates a misuse of ascorbic acid.
Fruit		You may have noticed that in a good white wine, especially in a sweet one, the fruit aromas evolve as the wine matures. They become almost jammy and take on the smells of compote, dried and stewed fruit.
	Lemon	An elegant perfume that lightens the bouquet and gives the wine a freshness.
	Apricot Peach	You are likely to find these odors in top white wines of considerable strength meant for aging, and in sweet wines.
	Blackcurrant Raspberry Small red fruit	The typical and easily recognizable principal smells found in red wines meant for early drinking and in those red wines meant for aging that are drunk when young.
	Blackberry Mulberry	The original odor associated with quality in reds.
	Quince Strawberry	Depending on the grape variety and the soil type, these perfumes can be evident in a wine maturing or on the decline.
	Bergamot Lemon Orange Tangerine	These are powerful and elegant smells and are very charac-teristic of Muscatel-like for-tified wines. Also found in Australian Rieslings and in the Sémillon grape.

FAMILY OF SMELLS	EXAMPLES	COMMENTS
	Cherry Redcurrants	A subtle perfume that is considered a good odor. Think Cabernet Sauvignon or Pinot Noir.
	Apple	Can be either a good or a bad thing. If it smells like an overripe apple or beet, it is a sign of oxidation or problematic malolactic fermentation. If it smells like a golden or green apple in a young, dry white wine, then it is good.
	Banana Pear	When there is too much of this smell it almost resembles nail polish. It is a very simple odor usually found in white wines of little originality whose fermentations were jump-started with industrial-flavored yeasts, in Primeur red wines, and in "technological" rosés.
	Plum Raisin	These are pretty rare in wines. You might detect them in some young, simple reds.
	Guava Kiwi Lychee Papaya Passion fruit	Considered to be original and agreeable smells, if not too strong, in certain white wines (Gewürztraminer, for example).
Nuts and dried fruit	Hazelnut Roasted almond	These are considered to be aromas of great class, especially when present in the tertiary bouquet of the top, well-built and solid white wines such as a mature white Burgundy.
	Dried fig Walnut	Very classic aromas found in aged, fortified wines as well as in top wines at their peak of maturity.

FAMILY OF SMELLS	EXAMPLES	COMMENTS
	Prunes	A bad sign. This usually means that a red wine has faded or died, or is an indication that there was a problem with oxidation, probably due to bad storage or conservation conditions.
Vegetable	Cut grass Herbaceous Stalk or stems	Considered a bad thing, these smells are usually the result of bad harvesting practices, grapes that are too crushed or not destalked well. You also find these odors in technological wines that are past their prime.
	Fern	A very distinguished odor that is found in white and red wines meant for long-term aging.
	Cut hay	A nice odor present in certain red wines.
	Juniper Incense Pine Resin Turpentine	These are powerful perfumes that are found in red wines from regions of southern or meridian climates, of pine forests.
	Humus Lichen Marsh Mushroom Undergrowth Wet straw	Considered to be desirable odors, they are linked to the phenomenon of reduction in the bottle and so are found in top red wines that have undergone a number of years of bottle aging.
	Dry leaves Herbal infusion Tea Tisane or herbal tea Tobacco	These smells usually indicate a certain amount of aging and evolution, and are found in both red and white wines meant for aging.
	Mint Eucalyptus	Characteristic smells of Cabernet Sauvignon grown in Australia, South Africa, or California.

FAMILY OF SMELLS	EXAMPLES	COMMENTS
	Dust Earth	Not considered desirable, these odors usually disappear with a little airing.
	Green pepper	The dominant odor usually associated with a young Cabernet Sauvignon or Cabernet Franc wine. If too strong, it means that the grapes were harvested while underripe.
Spices and herbs	Basil Bay Cinnamon Lavender Nutmeg Thyme	Powerful odors found in red wines and certain mature white wines issued from vintages of substantial warmth and sunshine.
	Licorice Pepper	Considered very elegant and noble, these aromas are often present in the best reds from the best *terroirs*.
	Aniseed Cloves Fennel	In small amounts, these are acceptable smells.
	Garlic Onions	Not so good. Usually means that the wine suffered reduction in the bottle.
	Vanilla	A very pleasant perfume that can bring balance and harmony to the wine if not overpowering. Usually found in wines that have been aged in new oak barrels.
	Truffle	A very strong odor that can sometimes resemble aspects of the vegetable family (underwood and humus), or even the animal family (sweat, urine). If present in old wines, it is an expression of quality— but the wine definitely needs aeration if you are to fully appreciate it.

FAMILY OF SMELLS	EXAMPLES	COMMENTS
Animal	Amber Civet (cat) Musk	These three are powerful and surprising odors that are usually appreciated if they are found in well-developed, aged, and evolved red wines.
	Game	A very powerful aroma usually found in very old red wines—Pommards can definitely smell a bit gamey.
	Cat urine	Found in Sauvignon Blanc grapes that were picked while underripe, or yields were too high.
	Fur Game Leather Sweat Wet dog	A very particular odor appreciated by those who go in for this sort of thing. Found in great red wines after a long and perfect maturation.
	Chicken gut Fox	Bad smells associated with wines that have been poorly vinified or are from hybrid grape varieties.
Roasted	Burnt Grilled Smoke Toast	Can be lovely when found in some white wines of distinction. Aged white Burgundies often have these notes.
	Cocoa Chocolate Coffee	Very desirable aromas found in the top red wines when at their apogee.
	Burnt wood Creosote Rubber Smoke Tar	Characteristic odors of certain red wines while in the process of maturation. They often disappear once the wine is fully mature.
	Caramel	A heady, heavy perfume, like the quince, usually indicates that the wine is maturing too quickly or that it was vinified at too high a temperature.

FAMILY OF SMELLS	EXAMPLES	COMMENTS
	Flint Gunpowder	Typical of dry white wines of the Loire Valley. A very pleasing smell and taste that is said to be due to flinty soil.
	Honey Wax	Lovely perfumes that develop in mature white wines of great class.
	Acetate Nail polish	Disagreeable smells found in poorly made young red wines or technological rosés.
	Beer Cheese Cider Dirty dishcloth Milk Sauerkraut Yeast Yogurt	A whole pack of not-so-lovely odors that are all caused by poorly managed fermentations.
	Cattle shed Mold Pigsty Soap Stagnation	Again, odors considered not so good and that are linked to poor quality.
Alcohol	*Eau de vie* Kirsch Old marc	Perfumes present in very heady wines rich in alcohol.
	Graphite Iodine	Sometimes found in wine and not considered to be good signs.

Translated and adapted from *La Dégustation*, pp. 48–53, G. Gribourg and C. Sarfati, Edisud, France 1989.

THE GRAPES

All the factors we have looked at are important in telling you about the taste of a wine, but the single most important factor is the grape variety or varieties from which the wine is made. In winemaking, just as in cooking, if you use inferior raw materials and do not adjust the proportions of the ingredients correctly, your final dish will fall short of the mark.

Do not forget that the grape is a fruit or a crop like any other, and crops come from different regions for a reason. Bananas come from the Tropics, figs from the Mediterranean, apples from temperate areas like the U.S. and Canada. It would be foolhardy to try to grow these fruits in places other than their indigenous habitat or where the growing conditions are totally different. They might survive, but they would probably not be as good. So why do we do it with the noble European grape varieties? The Chardonnay grape is at its optimum in Burgundy, as is the Cabernet Sauvignon in Médoc and Graves, the Merlot in St-Emilion or Pomerol, the Kékfrankos in Sopron, Hungary, the Nebbiolo in Piedmont, and the Tempranillo in Rioja. There are even indigenous grape varieties in some of the New World countries. However, there is debate that even these have European roots. For example, California's Zinfandel, although considered indigenous if not very old and settled, is of Italian origin from the Primitivo grape. South Africa's Pinotage is a hybrid of France's Cinsault and Pinot Noir varieties, and Australia's Shiraz is the Rhône Valley's Syrah. In any event, they are grapes that have been there long enough to have taken on a personality that reflects the region's soil and climate. They all make delicious and unique wines.

When noble European grape varieties are grown in new, adopted soils, they produce different tastes and styles, usually as a result of the warmer climate. Once I would have argued that not only were these new models different, but they were also inferior. I would not say so today. It is simply that it is too soon to know how these varieties will settle into their new environment. It is unfair to compare a vineyard that has been producing fruit for hundreds of years, such as Chablis (100 percent Chardonnay grapes by law), with one that has only been doing so for a couple of decades. It will take ages for nature to sort out the myriad variables that are best suited: which grapes with which soil, which climate, and so on.

You also have to decide whether or not you accept a new and different perception of the classic model. Should we accept that the Chardonnay grape could have a Chablis (Burgundy) taste, a Carneros (California) taste, or a Maipo (Chile) taste? And even more to the point, is there a significant difference between a California and a Chilean Chardonnay? Or are all Chardonnays of the New World subject to, and thus products of, the same technical and climatic treatments? For you to decide!

Not All Grapes Can Go It Alone

Some grape varieties—despite occasional flirtations—do very well on their own: Pinot Noir, Sauvignon Blanc, Riesling, Chardonnay. Others are best when blended with other grape varieties: Merlot, Cabernet Sauvignon, Cabernet Franc.

Why? Take Bordeaux wines as an example, where Cabernet Sauvignon is the main ingredient of the recipe. Merlot, because it is a sweeter and softer grape than the Cabernet Sauvignon, has traditionally been used to soften the tannins of the Cabernet Sauvignon. Cabernet Franc is also added as the spice of the recipe, giving its own special character, plus there are minute doses of Petit Verdot and/or Malbec. Combining the taste elements of all the varieties gives each Bordeaux appellation its unique flavor.

Each appellation has a designated recipe according to which grape varieties do better in that area because of the soil and microclimate. And within this recipe, each winemaker makes his or her own variations according to which grapes did better than another in any particular year, and according to the personal tastes of the château owner and winemaker. In the same way, when cooking, we follow a basic recipe yet will vary the proportion of ingredients (meat, vegetables, spices, and flavorings) according to our personal taste, the seasonal availability of ingredients, and perhaps our financial resources.

The Style Parameters of the Grape Varieties

Every grape variety produces grapes that have a specific chemical constitution and therefore possess a particular aromatic potential, in varying degrees of intensity and quality. Some varieties are considered to have no interest at all; these are usually hybrids. The varieties considered rich in primary aromas, such as Muscat, Gewürztraminer, or Riesling, produce wines that taste as though you've just bitten into a grape. These are the varieties that are vinified in such a way as to preserve or amplify these aromas.

Then there are the varieties susceptible to an aromatic potential of interesting secondary aromas: Gamay, Pinot Noir, Marsanne, Cabernet Sauvignon, Grenache, Chardonnay, Syrah, and Chenin. Only vinification can reveal the hidden aromatic potential of these grapes.

Finally, we have those varieties that develop through vinification and continue to evolve with aging: Pinot Noir, Cabernet Sauvignon, and Syrah, for example. Take a Gamay from Beaujolais and a Pinot Noir from Burgundy, and it will be the Pinot Noir that will still taste amazing after sitting in your cellar for five or ten years, not the Gamay, no matter what a winemaker does to it. Each grape variety has a finite aromatic and taste potential.

A grape variety, from the start, is either meant for aging or not. There are varieties that produce wines with a balance of sugar, acid, and tannin—which gives them the structure needed to sustain aging. Then there are varieties that produce wines that are meant to be drunk while young, as they reveal themselves best while still youthful, and whose sugar, acid, tannin balance is relatively light.

Winemakers can try to squeeze as much as they like out of grapes by letting them overproduce and by extracting as much flavor during the vinification as possible. For example, to get the most out of a variety that does not have much aroma, such as the Ugni Blanc, a winemaker can vinify the must, or grape juice, with little or no oxidation and at very low temperatures, thus eking out a little more flavor. But this will only be a superficial result. Nature has provided built-in limits.

To make a grape happy, all you need to do is provide a perfect environment. In its optimum site of acclimation—the place where the soil, climate, and growing conditions are all perfect—each variety will find its optimum individual and specific sugar, acid, and tannin balance. For example, in Alsace, the Gewürztraminer will always be sweeter than the Riesling. In the Côtes du Rhône, Carignan will always be more acidic than Grenache, and in Burgundy, Pinot Noir will always be more tannic than Gamay. In the right region and conditions, each grape variety is reaching its own taste potential.

THE WHITE GRAPES

To help you identify grape varieties, here is a list of the major white grapes and their characteristics.

White wine grape varieties generally smell and taste like citrus and other tree fruit, like lemon, orange, grapefruit, or apple. In mature white wines, or in sweet white wines, we often taste more exotic or tropical fruit, like pineapple, mango, apricot, pear, melon, and lychee.

Both red and white wines can have odors and tastes such as mineral, spice, herbs, tobacco, hay, yeast, honey, caramel, and nuts. The tastes come from either the grape variety, the yeasts (if indigenous yeasts are not used to start fermentation), the fermentation period, or the oak used for aging.

Chardonnay

An easygoing kind of grape, the Chardonnay seems to want to please everyone. It does its best to adapt to every soil, every climate of every country, and every winemaking style. Who would believe that the same grape could give us a wine that is steely, mineral, and salty as well as one that's fat, buttery, oaky, and lightly sweet? But the Chardonnay does just that. And nowhere are its many personalities better illustrated than in the *marno-calcaires* soils of Burgundy. Indeed, Burgundy is the perfect region in which to observe varietal variations and provides a strong defense for the unique variable of soil type. From the cool climate and *calcaire* soil of Chablis to the warmer Mâcon, the Chardonnay adapts perfectly, becoming more aromatic and supple as it moves farther south. Take it out of its native Burgundy altogether and it quickly becomes attuned to its adopted land's climate and environment.

Chardonnays from northern Italy and southern France are both light and fruity; those from Chile are vibrant with fruit and light oak; from New Zealand's cooler regions, the wines become intense with balanced fruit; and from California, they are tropical, rich wines.

Chenin Blanc

Good Chenin Blanc is one of the world's most underrated grape varieties. It is true that Chenin Blanc from a very cold year can produce a sour wine, but with a little sunshine, its true colors are revealed. This happens best in its home, the Loire Valley. The Chenin Blanc has several very distinct sides to it. When harvested at optimum maturity, it produces a dry, firm, elegantly floral wine, such as a Savennières. It also produces sparkling wines of good quality in Saumur and Vouvray. When harvested late so that noble rot *(selection de grains nobles)* is successfully achieved—when the grapes are deliberately allowed to shrivel and intensify on the vine before harvesting—then the most succulent and famous sweet wines are the result: Coteaux du Layon, Bonnezeaux, and Quarts de Chaume, all apples and apricots with nutty, honey tones and underlined by a high acidity that helps carry it all along. These are long lived, but not as fat or ageless as a Sauternes.

Outside the Loire Valley and into warmer climates, Chenin Blanc unfortunately becomes a fairly innocuous thing. New World versions are at best fruity, but lacking any of its crucial steeliness or complexity. Nor does this grape lend itself to high yields: Overproduction is truly merciless. Having realized this, the South Africans and others are starting to nurture older vines in an attempt to get more concentrated and complex fruit (older plants give fewer, more concentrated grapes, while younger plants produce higher yields of lighter fruit).

Gewürztraminer

There is no more distinctive or aromatic grape than the Gewürztraminer. Alsace is its home and there it produces, if yields are kept reasonably low, a rich tapestry of fruity, floral, and spicy tastes. Its texture in the mouth is round, rich, and smooth. Like the Riesling, it can be harvested late *(vendanges tardives)* to produce a very classy wine; in certain years, when the weather is perfect and noble rot is attained, the results are amazing. Although often described as "spicy," the first impression is frequently of roses and lychees. When made in the dry style, it is still opulent but it does not fare well in warm years or warm climates, where the heat lets its acid levels plummet, leaving it overly sweet, oily, and flabby.

Germany's Pfalz and Baden regions run a close second to Alsace, and lighter versions come from Austria and Italy's Sudtirol. Outside Europe, the wines are usually off dry, easy, and without much character. But growers who take it seriously in cooler climates such as Washington State and Oregon are producing some great results.

Marsanne

Native of the mid–Rhône Valley, this variety is one of the Rhône Valley Hermitage staples, and when coupled with Roussanne produces Hermitage, Crozes-Hermitage at St-Joseph. It has also been planted farther south in France and in Australia. When young, it is a discreet wine that becomes more floral as it ages, moving toward notes of wax, honey, and nuts. On the palate, the wines are supple, fat, and round.

Müller-Thurgau

A cross between Riesling and Silvaner. Its creator, Dr. Hermann Müller of Germany, was trying to combine the quality of the Riesling grape with the reliability of the Silvaner. Since Silvaner is an early-maturing grape, it is very popular in cold vine-growing regions, as it matures before the worst weather arrives. But Müller-Thurgau turned out to make a rather flabby, mediocre wine, especially when a product of Germany's high yields. It does much better in New Zealand, Washington State, some parts of Italy, and is the variety most commonly grown in England. At its best, it charms us with its floral scents of privet and flowering currant leaves.

Muscat

You may have noticed that most grapes taste of everything but grapes as we have always thought of them. Muscat is a grape-tasting grape and is also one of the oldest grape varieties in the world. Alsatian Muscats are elegant, dry, rose-scented wines, usually drunk as an aperitif. The very sweet, fortified Muscats of the south of France and the Rhône (Frontignan, Lunel, Rivesaltes, and Beaumes-de-Venise) are drunk with desserts. Australia produces darker, heavier liqueur Muscats of high quality. Italy's fizzy, low-alcohol, sweet Moscatos, such as Asti Spumante, are refreshing and versatile, and who can ignore the delectable Moscatel de Setúbal from Portugal?

Pinot Blanc

You may think that the Pinot Blanc is an innocuous little grape, but it has quite a lot to say for itself, which is difficult for a grape that is a mutation of a mutation. The Pinot Blanc, originally from Burgundy, is a white mutation of the Pinot Gris, which is a mutation of the Pinot Noir! The Germans, French, and Italians have long appreciated its startling resemblance to light, unoaked Chardonnay. Indeed, this resemblance is physical as well as gustative, as it is very difficult to tell the plant vines apart. A well-made Pinot Blanc will remind you of apples, butter, and warm, sweet sap. The Alsatian version contributes something to almost every meal, its delicacy present yet discreet.

Pinot Gris

Pinot Gris, as I have just mentioned, is a mutation of the Pinot Noir grape, and comes in many packages and under several names, but it finds its full expression in Alsace, where it is known as Tokay Pinot Gris, although the Hungarians are insisting that Tokay be dropped from the name so there is no confusion with their famous Tokàji. It skirts seductively between the steeliness of the Riesling and the spicy voluptuousness of the Gewürztraminer, never making up its mind. It is smoky, spicy, nougatty. At the other extreme, it produces a light, dry wine, the Pinot Grigio, in Italy.

Riesling

The true Riesling of German origin is one of the world's great grape varieties. Like Sauvignon Blanc, it has both a strong personality—one that is better off without the influence of oak—and high acidity, but it is far more adaptable. It thrives in the cool climates of Europe, especially in Germany and Alsace and, to some extent, the warmer climates of Australia, although high yields in such a climate can render it soapy. It is very susceptible to noble rot, which means that it can produce wines in many styles, from the dry to the intensely sweet. Because of their high acidity and sugar levels, Rieslings can age for many years. Wherever it is grown, whether it is old or young, and no matter which wine style it has produced, you should always be able to detect a vivid fruitiness and a lively acidity. If too sweet, it loses its personality and becomes heavy and cloying. It should sing to you of honeysuckle, crunchy green apples, spiced baked apples, quince and orange, and of that famous tarry aroma.

Sauvignon Blanc

This grape is responsible for many of France's great white wines: from the gorgeously noble Sauternes and its many sisters (Barsac, Cadillac, Ste-Croix-du-Mont, Loupiac) to the crisp, elegant, and delicate Sancerre with its steely, stony, white-flower aromas typical of the Loire Valley's flint soils. Transported to other soils, it is quite transformed; perhaps that is why it is rarely recognized. New Zealand's refreshing version is an explosion of gooseberries, freshly cut grass, and tropical fruit. Be careful if you detect the lingering odor of canned asparagus, green beans, or an exaggerated herbaceousness—almost a stemminess—as these are considered, not surprisingly, to be undesirable and are certainly due to too-high yields.

Sémillon

One member of the trio of the famous white Bordeaux blend (Sauvignon Blanc, Muscadelle, and Sémillon), Sémillon makes unforgettable sweet white wines—Sauternes, Barsac, Cadillac, and so on—and, of course, the dry white Bordeaux, the Graves, and Pessac-Léognan. There is a good reason that it is usually part of a blend, as on its own it creates a dry white wine that is at best lightly citrus-fruity, slightly herbaceous like the Sauvignon Blanc, but usually lacking originality. Heavily oaked, as in the Barossa Valley, it produces a fat, vanilla, lemony wine. It has won great acclaim for its results in an unusual dry white from Australia's Hunter Valley. Other New World countries have married it to Chardonnay to pad out the yield shortages of the extremely popular Chardonnay grape.

Ugni Blanc

A grape possessing many names and roles—surprisingly, considering its lack of distinction and originality. Or perhaps, this is just what makes it the perfect candidate for ubiquitousness. Known as Ugni Blanc, Clairette Ronde, and Muscadet in Aigre in France, and as Trebbiano in Italy, whence it originates. Legend has it that Ugni Blanc was brought to southern France during the fourteenth century, probably via Avignon, the seat of the papal court. It is the most planted variety in both France and Italy, stealing its way into all of our favorite Provençal, Rhône, and Bordeaux blends—not to mention its importance in brandy. This is because it will grow vigorously, providing high yields, in almost any warm-climate conditions, withstanding disease and rot. At best, as a varietal, it makes a light, white, and crisp wine that's low in alcohol and high in acidity. At worst, it is boring and tasteless.

Viognier

Native to the Condrieu region of the Rhône Valley, this grape is the stuff of heady, perfumed, yet dry, full-bodied opulence. It is all lime blossoms, musk, apricots, and peaches. On the palate, it is well rounded and mellow, despite its high acidity and alcohol content, making it a wine of great class. However, it is considered unreliable and needs to reach a perfect maturity in order to express itself fully. This is best assured when it is planted on the south-facing slopes of the Rhône Valley. Still, if the weather is not right, there is no crop at all—and even when all goes according to plan, the yields are low, which means high prices. Also grown in Languedoc-Roussillon and California with excellent results, it has been designated a trendy new grape.

THE RED GRAPES

Now let's look at the characteristics of the major red grape varieties.

Red wine grape varieties generally taste like the red fruit family: black and red cherry, redcurrant and blackcurrant, raspberry, strawberry, and plum.

As you have seen, both red and white wines can have odors and tastes such as minerals, spices, herbs, tobacco, hay, yeast, honey, caramel, and nuts. The tastes come from either the grape variety, the yeasts (if indigenous yeasts are not used to start fermentation), the fermentation period, or the oak used for aging.

Barbera

Usually part of a blend, the most valuable contribution of the Barbera grape is its naturally high acidity. Hailing originally from Piedmont, it is best matched with grapes of higher tannin content and body (such as its nemesis Nebbiolo), as it produces red wines lighter in style and earlier maturing than Barolo, with pronounced astringency. Because of its high acidity, it does well in warm and hot climates. It has been very successfully grown in Argentina, where it produces a warm, juicy, and intense wine with strong undertones of its typical sour cherry notes. It is also very popular in California's hot Central Valley because of this high acidity.

Cabernet Franc

Another blending grape, this variety adds a touch of spice and reliability (it matures easily in all weathers) to the formidable Bordeaux blend (usually no more than 20 to 25 percent), along with Cabernet Sauvignon and Merlot (and traces of Petit Verdot and Malbec). Although it would not stand a chance as a single variety in Bordeaux (although we should not forget the Château Cheval Blanc, 66 percent Cabernet Franc, 33 percent Merlot, 1 percent Malbec), it totally holds its own in the Loire Valley, where it offers us the aromatic, tannic, red-fruity Saumur-Champigny, Bourgueil, and Chinon. It does well in cool, inland climates, and produces fabulous results in Argentina, New York State's Long Island, and New Zealand. One place it is not really suited for is the overly warm Napa Valley, where it was planted in order to obtain the Californian "Bordeaux" blend Meritage. I also must add that I have enjoyed several spicy, personable, and intense bottles from Hungary.

Cabernet Sauvignon

The Cabernet Sauvignon grape, like the Chardonnay, has become one of those overtransported, overplanted, abused grape varieties victimized by the trendsetters of the New World. The result is that there are so many versions of this grape that we forget what it does best: a trio act, in Bordeaux. Yes, it is adaptable, but it shouldn't be made to perform every trick under the sun. Under ideal climatic conditions, it produces an aromatic, tannic wine that ages and evolves elegantly yet powerfully. If harvested when underripe or with enormous yields, the results can be truly mediocre: The wine too tannic and light bodied with violent green pepper and herbaceous odors. If the climate is too warm and the grapes are overripe, the resulting wines can have very jammy, baked, fortified flavors and will lack structure. A perfectly balanced Bordeaux is what we are after and, if achieved, it will have notes of blackcurrants, cedar, cigars, lead pencils, green pepper, mint, and dark chocolate. Sounds delicious.

Gamay

Gamay is a native of the granite soils of Beaujolais, and if you truly know how this grape variety works, you will understand why Beaujolais Nouveau is best drunk immediately—and I mean within a few days! It was the grape variety deemed too common by the medieval king Philip the Bold, who demanded that all the Gamay on the Côte d'Or be uprooted in favor of the "nobler" Pinot Noir of Burgundy. But the peasants working the vineyards insisted on keeping a few plantings, as that was what they relied upon to give them sustenance. Because it was considered inferior and because it was not treated seriously, it was drunk before it could even be bottled. It is true that when Gamay is given a very short *cuvaison* (the time spent in the vat) and is of a high yield, it produces Primeur wines that are light but fresh and very aromatic with notes of red fruit and bananas.

However, I am always reminded of an aftertaste of a copper coin. When allowed to macerate longer, as with the Crus of Beaujolais—wines from ten specially designated villages—the wine can be very well rounded, elegant, and enjoyable.

Grenache

Although originally from Spain, this grape is best known for its great works in France's Rhône Valley: Châteauneuf-du-Pape, Appellation Contrôlée Côtes du Rhône, Gigondas, and so on. Again, here is a grape variety that is best used as a blend (with Syrah, Cinsault, and Mourvèdre), but is often used as a single variety in southern France and in the New World. When not of high yields, the wine has a dark robe, is rather aromatic, and has notes of pepper, raspberries, and herbs, with supple acids, a round, fat texture, generous alcohols, and a rustic edge. When yields are too high, the wine is light colored and tastes a bit oxidized, or like cheap cherry bonbons. It is very popular in South Africa, Australia, and California because it is susceptible to rot and mildew and thus is better suited to dry climates.

Malbec

Again, a grape variety that is used in the red Bordeaux blend, where the Cabernet Sauvignon, Cabernet Franc, and Merlot dominate its personality. However, this dark, tannic grape (also called Auxerrois) comes into its own in southwestern France, where it can be a major component in the lushly rustic, dark, and brooding Cahors, Buzet, Bergerac, Côtes de Duras, Côtes du Frontonnais, Côtes du Marmandais, and Pécharmant. In Argentina, it produces the best reds: velvety, vigorous, aromatic, and worthy of cellar aging. In Chile, it tends to be blended with the softer Merlot and is gorgeous. Almost anywhere it is grown, Malbec seems to retain its lovely tastes of blackberries, blackcurrants, lavender, and spices.

Merlot

In the red Bordeaux blend, I like to think of the Merlot as the sugar in the recipe, the Cabernet Sauvignon as the flour, and the Cabernet Franc as the spices. Merlot gives softer, plumper, and juicy, early-maturing wines that are sweeter; a perfect complement to the tannic Cabernet Sauvignon and the spicy Cabernet Franc. The Merlot tastes of plums, roses, blackcurrants, and rich fruitcake. There are in Bordeaux appellations where the bulk of the blend is Merlot based, such as Pomerol and St-Emilion. As an unblended varietal wine it does well in California; the warmer climate accentuates its natural sweet suppleness and thus gives it commercial appeal. However, I find that most of the Merlots grown in warm climates and served up as single varieties lack structure, acid, and character. It needs the company of other grapes to show off its potential, as hotter climates do bring out its spicier, plummier side, but the allure is a superficial one. It produces light, grassy wines in northern Italy, and if blended does well in New Zealand and South Africa. Chile also seems to get it to stand rather well on its own.

Mourvèdre

Originally a Spanish grape, known there as Monastrelli, its robust aromas are better known in Provence's Bandol region and in the Rhône Valley, where it is often blended with Syrah and Grenache. The south of France has embraced it as one of its trendy varietals. It does best in hot climates, where its tastes of blackberries, game, and leather can be appreciated. Because it is a rather tannic, highly colored, and robust grape, its wines need aging, which will further enhance its wild, gamey character. South Australia and California (as a "Rhône Ranger") are both doing good things with it.

Nebbiolo

The small, thick-skinned Nebbiolo grape produces some of the driest, biggest, and toughest of intense red wines, capable of long bottle aging. When well made and matured, it is a magical confusion of prunes, tar, licorice, violets, roses, chocolate, and spicy fruitcake. Its stronghold is Piedmont and thereabouts in northwest Italy, where its two most famous wines are Barolo and Barbaresco. It is rare outside Italy and this is probably a very good thing, as other versions tend to be uninteresting and harsh.

Periquita

This is a versatile grape variety native to southern Portugal. It has five or six other names, all of them unpronounceable and impossible to spell. It was named Periquita (small parrot) by José Maria da Fonseca after his small farm, where he started his winemaking operation. I guess he, too, found the other names too difficult to spell! It is often dismissed as very ordinary, but I think it makes a most original wine. It has a silky texture and full-bodied sweetness, yet is powerful with a pleasant bite. If you want a taste of Portugal, try the indigenous grape varieties, not the ubiquitous Chardonnays and Cabernet Sauvignons. There are hundreds more grape varieties in Portugal, all capable of creating the most characterful brews.

Pinot Noir

When asked if I prefer Bordeaux or Burgundy, I quickly jump at the chance to enthuse passionately about the seductive superiority of the Pinot Noir. When grown correctly (cool climate, small yields), a Burgundy reaches the pinnacle of sophistication and elegance so often associated with the Bordeaux, but then surpasses it, flaunting its sexy, animal-like charm. The Burgundy seems to overflow exuberantly, while the Bordeaux, however moving, always seems a bit restrained in comparison. It is the mature Pinot Noir's complex flavors of raspberries, strawberries, cranberries, violets, game, compost, allspice, tobacco, and hay, coupled with its silky, velvety texture, that are so captivating. Pinot Noir is the most precocious of the fine-wine grapes to grow and vinify. Relatively low in tannin and acidity, it needs a cool climate. Too little sun leads to pallid, thin-tasting wine. With too much warmth, Pinot Noir can develop jammy, baked flavors, losing its elegance and silkiness. Even the best New World Pinot Noirs lack the magical complexity of the greatest Burgundies, where it is perfectly at home in the *argilo-calcaire* soils and cool climate.

Pinotage

Considered an indigenous grape variety of South Africa, this is actually a cross between Pinot Noir and Cinsault (since 1926). It produces everything from light, fruity wines to robust, distinctive, and hearty reds with strong tannic backbones and flavors of plums, brambles, flambéed bananas, and smoky oak. One of the best offerings from South Africa, it is a lovely, original-tasting grape variety.

Sangiovese

Taste a Sangiovese (blood of Jove) and you will immediately conjure images of Italy. As the major component of the famous Chianti wine (along with Cannaiolo Nero, Trebbiano, and Malvasia del Chianti), it is actually grown all over Italy. Naturally tannic, it is best used in a blend, usually with Cabernet Sauvignon, although on its own it shines as the delicious Rosso di Montalcino and Rosso di Montepulciano. As with the other late-maturing grape varieties we have seen (Grenache and Mourvèdre), it needs a hot climate in order to produce the richness and alcohol content required for bottle aging. In cooler climates, it tends to have sharp acids and bitter tannins. It is a very rich, robust wine that will do well with long bottle aging. Styles vary from light, astringent, and ordinary to a full-bodied, firm, slightly spicy red (with bitter cherry, tobacco, and herb flavors). It is becoming very popular in the New World, especially in California, where it is often blended with Cabernet Sauvignon.

Syrah

Called Shiraz in Australia and South Africa, Syrah is the magic varietal behind the Rhône Valley's famous Hermitage, Côte Rôtie, Cornas, St-Joseph, and Crozes-Hermitage. At home in the valley's granite soils, it produces wines that are deep in color and aroma. When young, they display floral and fruity (raspberry) notes. Once matured, this evolves into notes of black pepper, leather, spices, and game. Syrah is a very versatile grape and can be grown in almost any climate, although yields need to be kept down and overripeness must be avoided or the wine can become heavy, flabby, and too tannic. Some winemakers then fall into the trap of harvesting when the grapes are not at all mature, which gives equally mediocre results. Outside France, in Australia and California, Syrah is used both as a single variety and in blends with good results.

Tempranillo

Often labeled Spain's Cabernet Sauvignon, Tempranillo is the mainstay of most of its reds. It does well in its native Rioja because it is not too high in alcohol or acidity, despite the hot climate. These are rich, dark grapes that make wine capable of bottle aging. We know it best as an oaky (often overoaked!), mellow, sultry, vanilla-rich red. Without oak, its fruity notes are more evident.

Zinfandel

Considered the indigenous grape variety of California, the Zinfandel has finally been established as the same as the Primitivo of southern Italy, which means that it is one of many varieties that made it to the New World via an immigrant's suitcase. In California, it became best known back in the 1970s and 1980s as a white Zinfandel—so much so that most consumers assumed it was a white grape and not red! After the "blush" trend faded, winemakers started producing more red Zinfandel. A good Zinfandel is robust, spicy, blackberry-ish, interesting, and, in my opinion, by far the most individual variety coming out of California. If yields are respected and the grapes are grown in cooler hillside regions, the results are worth cellaring for many years.

WHICH GRAPES MAKE WHICH WINES?

What follows is a list of geographically named wines. It is not necessary to be exhaustive here, as the topic of grape varieties could fill another book; indeed, if you turn to the works of Jancis Robinson, you will be in very good hands! This list contains some of the better-known wine names, including those referred to in the cross-references of part 3.

When learning about the wines of a particular region, it is often simpler to start with the grape varieties that are grown in each appellation (regulated by law) than to memorize the wine names, not knowing of what they are comprised. Why is it important to know which grape varieties have been used? Because it will help you find wines that you like. Often the same grape variety has different names in different countries; you might be surprised to see a grape you know from the south of France in some far-flung corner of Italy. Or you may find that you consistently prefer a Blanc de Blancs to a Blanc de Noirs Champagne. This means that you prefer Champagne issued from the Chardonnay rather than the Pinot Noir and Pinot Meunier grapes. Then you can choose sparkling wines from other countries, or (because the two grapes truly produce different tastes) you will be better able to match them to food.

The grape varieties for each wine are listed in order of proportion; the first variety is often 50 percent or more of the blend. I listed all of them where space permitted, even if only traces of the grape are used in the wine, simply because I thought it interesting. Where there were too many grape varieties to list in this space, I resorted to using + or even ++.

NAME	REGION/ COUNTRY	COLOR/ STYLE	GRAPE VARIETIES
Ajaccio	Corsica, France	Red	Sciacarello, Grenache, Cinsault, Carignan
		White	Ugni Blanc, Vermentino Blanc
		Rosé	Barbarossa, Nielluccio, Sciacarello, Vermentino Blanc, Carignan, Cinsault, Grenache
Alenquer	Portugal	Red	Camarate, Mortagua, Periquita, Preto Martinho, Tinta Miuda
		White	Vital, Jampal, Arinto, Fernao Pires

NAME	REGION/ COUNTRY	COLOR/ STYLE	GRAPE VARIETIES
Almeirim	Portugal	Red	Castelao Nacional, Poeirinha, Periquita, Trincadeira Preta
		White	Fernao Pires, Arinto, Rabo de Ovelha, Talia, Trincadeira das Pratas, Vital
Aloxe Corton	Burgundy, France	Red	Pinot Noir
Amarone della Valpolicella	Veneto, Italy	Red	Corvina, Rondinella, Molinara
Anjou	Loire, France	Red	Cabernet Franc, Cabernet Sauvignon, Pineau d'Aunis (Chenin Noir)
		White	Chenin, Chardonnay, Sauvignon Blanc
		Rosé	Cabernet Franc, Cabernet Sauvignon, Gamay, Cot, Groslot
Apremont	Savoie, France	White	Jacquère, Chardonnay, Aligoté
Arbois	Jura, France	Red	Poulsard Noir, Trousseau, Pinot Noir
		White	Savagnin, Chardonnay, Pinot Blanc
Auxey Duresses	Burgundy, France	Red	Pinot Noir
		White	Chardonnay
Asti Spumante	Piedmont, Italy	Sparkling	Muscat (Moscato)
Bairrada	Portugal	Red	Baga, Castelao Frances, Tinta Pinheira
		White	Maria Gomes, Bical, Rabo de Ovelha
Bandol	Provence, France	Red	Mourvèdre, Grenache, Cinsault, Syrah, Tibouren, Calitor (Pecoui Touar)
		White	Bourboulenc, Clairette, Ugni Blanc, Sauvignon Blanc
		Rosé	Mourvèdre, Grenache, Cinsault, Syrah, Carignan, Tibouren, Calitor, Bourboulenc, Cairette, Ugni Blanc, Sauvignon Blanc
Banyuls	Roussillon	Vin doux naturel	Grenache Noir, Muscat
Barbaresco	Piedmont, Italy	Red	Nebbiolo Michet, Nebbiolo Lampia, Nebbiolo Rose
Barbera d'Asti	Piedmont, Italy	Red	Barbera, Freisa, Grignolino, Dolcetto
Bardolino	Veneto, Italy	Red	Corvina, Rondinella, Molinara, Negrara, Rossignola, Barbera, Sangiovese

NAME	REGION/ COUNTRY	COLOR/ STYLE	GRAPE VARIETIES
Barolo	Piedmont, Italy	Red	Nebbiolo Michet, Nebbiolo Lampia, Nebbiolo Rose
Barsac	Bordeaux	Sweet white	Sémillon, Sauvignon, Muscadelle
Bâtard-Montrachet	Burgundy	White	Chardonnay
Béarn	Southwest France	Red	Tannat, Cabernet Franc and Sauvignon, Fer, Manseng
Beaujolais	Burgundy, France	Red White	Gamay Chardonnay, Aligoté
Beaumes-de-Venise	Muscat de Rhône, France	*Vin doux naturel*	Muscat
Beaune	Burgundy, France	Red White	Pinot Noir Chardonnay
Bellet	Provence, France	Red White Rosé	Braquet, Folle Noir, Cinsault, Grenache, Rolle, Roussanne ++ Rolle, Roussanne, Spagnol, Clairette, Bourboulenc ++ Braquet, Folle Noir, Cinsault, Grenache, Roussanne ++
Bergerac	Dordogne, France	Red White	Cabernet Sauvignon, Cabernet Franc, Merlot, Malbec Sémillon, Sauvignon Blanc, Muscadelle
Bianco di Custoza	Veneto, Italy	White	Trebbiano Toscano, Garganega, Tocai Friulano, Cortese, Pinot Bianco, Chardonnay, Riesling Italico
Bianco di Scandiano	Emilia-Romagna, Italy	White	Sauvignon Blanc (Spergola)
Blanquette de Limoux	Languedoc, France	Sparkling	Mauzac, Chardonnay, Chenin
Bonnes Mares	Burgundy, France	Red	Pinot Noir
Bonnezeaux	Loire, France	Sweet white	Chenin Blanc
Botticino	Lombardy, Italy	Red	Barbera, Schiava Gentile, Marzemino, Sangiovese
Bourgueil	Loire, France	Red	Cabernet Franc

NAME	REGION/ COUNTRY	COLOR/ STYLE	GRAPE VARIETIES
Brouilly	Beaujolais, France	Red	Gamay
Brunello di Montalcino	Tuscany, Italy	Red	Sangiovese, Canaiolo, Trebbiano, Malvasia
Bull's Blood	Eger, Hungary	Red	Kékfrankos, Cabernet Sauvignon, Merlot
Buzet	Southwest France	Red	Merlot, Cabernet Sauvignon, Cabernet Franc, Malbec
		White	Sémillon, Sauvignon Blanc, Muscadelle
Cadillac	Bordeaux, France	Sweet white	Sémillon, Sauvignon, Muscadelle
Cahors	Southwest France	Red	Malbec, Merlot, Tannat, Jurançon Noir
Capri	Campania, Italy	Red	Piedirosso
		White	Falanghina, Greco, Biancolella
Cassis	Provence, France	Red/rosé	Grenache, Carignan, Mourvèdre, Cinsault, Barberoux ++
		White	Ugni Blanc, Sauvignon Blanc, Grenache Blanc, Marsanne ++
Cava	Spain	Sparkling	Xarel-lo, Parellada, Macabeo, Chardonnay
Chablis	Burgundy, France	White	Chardonnay
Chacoli de Guetaria	Northwest (Basque) Spain	Red White	Hondarribi Beltz Hondarribi Zuri
Chambertin	Burgundy, France	Red	Pinot Noir
Chambolle-Musigny	Burgundy, France	Red	Pinot Noir
Champagne	Champagne, France	Sparkling	Pinot Noir, Pinot Meunier or Chardonnay
Chassagne-Montrachet	Burgundy, France	White	Chardonnay
Châteauneuf-du-Pape	Rhône, France	Red	Grenache Noir, Cinsault, Syrah, Mourvèdre
		White	Grenache Blanc, Bourboulenc, Roussanne
Chianti	Tuscany, Italy	Red	Sangiovese, Canaiolo Nero, Trebbiano, Malvasia del Chianti

NAME	REGION/ COUNTRY	COLOR/ STYLE	GRAPE VARIETIES
Chinon	Loire, France	Red/rosé White	Cabernet Franc Chenin Blanc (Pineau de la Loire)
Clos de Vougeot	Burgundy, France	Red	Pinot Noir
Colli Orientali del Friuli	Friuli-Venezia Giulia	Red	Merlot, Cabernet Sauvignon, Pinot Nero
Condrieu	Rhône, France	White	Viognier
Corbières	Languedoc Roussillon	Red/rosé White	Carignan, Grenache, Cinsault ++ Roussanne Clairette, Grenache, Bourboulenc, Ugni Blanc, Maccabeau, Marsanne, Roussanne
Cornas	Rhône, France	Red	Syrah
Corton Charlemagne	Burgundy, France	White	Chardonnay
Corton	Burgundy, France	Red	Pinot Noir
Côte Rôtie	Rhône, France	Red White	Syrah Viognier
Coteaux d'Aix-en-Provence	Provence, France	Red/rosé White	Cabernet Sauvignon, Carignan, Cinsault, Cournoise, Grenache, Mourvèdre, Syrah Bourboulenc, Clairette, Grenache Blanc, Sauvignon Blanc, Sémillon, Ugni Blanc
Coteaux du Layon	Loire	Sweet white	Chenin Blanc
Côte de Beaune	Burgundy, France	Red	Pinot Noir
Côtes de Bourg	Bordeaux, France	Red White	Cabernet Sauvignon, Cabernet Franc, Merlot, Malbec Gros Verdot, Prolongeau Sauvignon Blanc, Sémillon, Muscadelle, Merlot Blanc, Colombard
Côtes de Duras	Southwest France	Red White	Cabernet Sauvignon, Cabernet Franc, Merlot, Malbec Sauvignon Blanc, Sémillon, Muscadelle, Chenin , Mauzac

NAME	REGION/ COUNTRY	COLOR/ STYLE	GRAPE VARIETIES
Côtes du Jura	Jura, France	Red	Poulsard Noir, Trousseau, Pinot Noir
		White	Sauvignon Blanc, Chardonnay, Pinot Blanc
Côtes de Montravel	Southwest France	White	Sémillon, Sauvignon Blanc, Muscadelle
Côtes de Provence	Provence, France	Red/rosé	Carignan, Cinsault, Grenache, Mourvèdre, Tibouren ++
		White	Clairette, Sémillon, Ugni Blanc, Vermentino Blanc/Rolle
Côte Chalonnaise	Burgundy, France	White	Chardonnay
		Red	Pinot Noir
Côte de Nuits	Burgundy, France	Red	Pinot Noir
		White	Chardonnay
Côtes du Rhône	Rhône, France	Red	Grenache Noir, Cinsault, Syrah, Mourvèdre, Pinot Noir, Gamay ++
		Rosé	Grenache Noir, Camarèse, Cinsault
		White	Clairette, Roussanne, Bourboulenc, Viognier, Picpoul, Marsanne ++
Côtes du Roussillon	Roussillon, France	Red/rosé	Carignan, Cinsault, Grenache, Lladoner Pelut Noir, Syrah, Mourvèdre, Maccabeau Blanc
		White	Grenache Blanc, Maccabeau Blanc, Tourbat Blanc, Marsanne, Roussanne
Côtes du St-Mont	Southwest France	Red/rosé	Tannat, Cabernet Sauvignon, Cabernet Franc, Merlot, Fer
		White	Arrufiac, Clairette, Courbu, Gros and Petit Manseng
Crémant d'Alsace	Alsace, France	Sparkling rosé	Pinot Noir
		Sparkling white	Riesling, Pinot Blanc, Chardonnay
Crémant de Bourgogne	Burgundy	Sparkling	Pinot Noir, Chardonnay, Pinot Gris, Pinot Blanc, Gamay, Aligoté

NAME	REGION/ COUNTRY	COLOR/ STYLE	GRAPE VARIETIES
Crémant de Loire	Loire, France	Sparkling	Chenin Blanc, Cabernet Franc, Cabernet Sauvignon, Pineau d'Aunis, Pinot Noir Chardonnay, Menu Pineau +
Crépy	Savoie, France	White	Chasselas
Crozes-Hermitage	Rhône, France	Red White	Syrah Marsanne, Rousanne
Dão	Portugal	Red White	Alfrocheiro Preto, Bastardo, Jaen, Tinta Pinheira, Tinta Barroca + Encruzado, Assario Branco, Barcelo, Borrado das Moscas
Dolcetto d'Alba	Piedmont, Italy	Red	Barbera
Echezeaux	Burgundy, France	Red	Pinot Noir
Entre-Deux-Mers	Bordeaux, France	White	Sémillon, Sauvignon Blanc, Muscadelle
Falerno del Massico	Campania, Italy	Red White	Aglianico, Piedirosso Falanghina
Fitou	Languedoc, France	Red	Carignan, Lladoner, Pelut, Grenache ++
Fleurie	Beaujolais, France	Red	Gamay
Frascati	Latium, Italy	White	Malvasia, Trebbiano
Fronsac	Bordeaux, France	Red	Merlot, Cabernet Franc, Cabernet Sauvignon, Malbec
Gaillac	Southwest France	Red/rosé White	Duras, Fer Sevadou, Gamay, Syrah, Cabs, Merlot + Len de L'El, Mauzac, Sémillon, Sauvignon Blanc ++
Gavi	Piedmont, Italy	White	Cortese
Gevrey-Chambertin	Burgundy, France	Red	Pinot Noir
Gigondas	Rhône, France	Red	Grenache Noir, Syrah, Mourvèdre
Grave del Friuli	Friuli-Venezia Giulia, Italy	Red White	Cabernet Franc, Cabernet Sauvignon Chardonnay, Pinot Bianco

NAME	REGION/ COUNTRY	COLOR/ STYLE	GRAPE VARIETIES
Graves	Bordeaux, France	Red	Cabernet Sauvignon, Cabernet Franc, Merlot
		White	Sémillon, Sauvignon Blanc, Muscadelle
Greco di Tufo	Campania, Italy	White	Greco, Falanghina, Biancolella
Hermitage	Rhône, France	Red	Syrah
		White	Marsanne, Roussanne
Irouléguy	Southwest France	Red/rosé	Cabernet Sauvignon, Cabernet Franc, Tannat
		White	Courbu, Manseng
Lambrusco di Sorbara	Emilia-Romagna, Italy	Red	Lambrusco di Sorbara, Lambrusco Salamino
L'Etoile	Jura, France	White	Chardonnay, Poulsard, Sauvignon Blanc
Lirac	Rhône, France	Red/rosé	Grenache Noir, Cinsault, Mourvèdre, Syrah, Carignan
		White	Clairette Blanc, Grenache Blanc, Bourboulenc, Ugni Blanc, Picpoul, Marsanne, Roussanne, Viognier
Limnos	Greece	White	Muscat of Alexandria
Loupiac	Bordeaux, France	Sweet white	Sémillon, Sauvignon Blanc, Muscadelle
Lugana	Lombardy, Italy	White	Trebbiano di Lugana
Mâcon	Burgundy, France	White	Chardonnay
Madiran	Southwest France	Red	Tannat, Cabernet Sauvignon, Cabernet Franc
Margaux	Bordeaux, France	Red	Cabernet Sauvignon, Cabernet Franc, Merlot, Carmenère, Malbec, Petit Verdot
Marino	Latium, Italy	White	Malvasia, Trebbiano
Marsala	Sicily, Italy	White	Grillo, Catarratto, Pignatello, Calabrese, Nerello
		Red	Mascalese, Inzolia, Nero d'Avola
Mercurey	Burgundy, France	Red	Pinot Noir
		White	Chardonnay
Meursault	Burgundy, France	White	Chardonnay

NAME	REGION/ COUNTRY	COLOR/ STYLE	GRAPE VARIETIES
Minervois	Languedoc, France	Red/rosé	Grenache, Syrah, Mourvèdre, Carignan, Lladoner Pelut Noir +
		White	Grenache Blanc, Bourboulenc Blanc, Maccabeau Blanc, Marsanne Blanche ++
Monbazillac	Bordeaux, France	Sweet white	Sémillon, Sauvignon Blanc, Muscadelle
Morgon	Beaujolais, France	Red	Gamay
Moulin-à-Vent	Beaujolais, France	Red	Gamay
Muscadet	Loire, France	White	Melon
Naoussa	Greece	Red	Xynomavro
Navarra	Spain	Red	Tempranillo, Garnacha Tinta, Cabernet Sauvignon, Merlot +
		White	Viura, Moscatel de Grano Menudo, Chardonnay, Garnacha Blanc +
Nemea	Greece	Red	Aghiorghitiko
Orvieto Abbocado	Umbria, Italy	White	Trebbiano Toscano, Verdello, Grechetto, Canailo Bianco, Malvasia Toscana
Pacherenc du Vic-Bilh	Southwest France	White	Arrufiac, Courbu, Gros and Petit Manseng
Palette	Provence, France	Red/rosé	Mourvèdre, Grenache, Cinsault ++
		White	Clairette à Gros Grains et Petits Grains, Ugni Blanc ++
Patrimonio	Corsica, France	Red/rosé	Nielluccio, Grenache, Sciacarello, Vermentino Blanc
		White	Vermentino Blanc, Ugni Blanc
Pauillac	Bordeaux, France	Red	Cabernet Sauvignon, Merlot, Cabernet Franc, Malbec, Petit Verdot
Pomerol	Bordeaux, France	Red	Cabernet Franc, Merlot, Cabernet Sauvignon
Pommard	Burgundy, France	Red	Pinot Noir

NAME	REGION/ COUNTRY	COLOR/ STYLE	GRAPE VARIETIES
Port	Portugal	Fortified red	Touriga Francesa, Touriga Nacianal, Bastardo, Mourisco, Tinto Cao ++
		Fortified white	Gouveio, Malvasia Fina, Rabigato, Viosinho, Donzelinho
Pouilly-sur-Loire	Loire, France	White	Chasselas/Sauvignon
Pouilly-Fuissé	Burgundy, France	White	Chardonnay
Pouilly-Fumé	Loire, France	White	Sauvignon Blanc
Puligny-Montrachet	Burgundy, France	White	Chardonnay
Quarts de Chaume	Loire, France	White	Chenin Blanc
Quincy	Loire, France	White	Sauvignon Blanc
Reguengos	Portugal	Red	Aragonez, Moreto, Periquita, Trincadeira
		White	Manteudo, Perrum, Rabo de Ovelha, Roupeiro
Ribeiro	Spain	Red	Caino, Garnacha, Ferron, Souson, Mencia, Tempranillo +
		White	Treixadura, Loureira, Albarino, Jerez ++
Richebourg	Burgundy, Frane	Red	Pinot Noir
Rioja	Spain	Red	Tempranillo, Garnacho
		White	Viura, Malvasia Riojana
Rueda	Spain	White	Verdejo, Viura, Sauvignon Blanc, Palomino Fino
Rosso di Montalcino	Tuscany, Italy	Red	Sangiovese
Rosso di Montepulciano	Tuscany, Italy	Red	Sangiovese, Canaiolo Nero
Rully	Burgundy, France	White	Chardonnay
		Red	Pinot Noir
St-Amour	Beaujolais, France	Red	Gamay
St-Emilion	Bordeaux, France	Red	Merlot, Cabernet Sauvignon, Cabernet Franc, Malbec
Ste-Croix-du-Mont	Bordeaux, France	Sweet white	Sémillon, Sauvignon Blanc, Muscadelle

NAME	REGION/ COUNTRY	COLOR/ STYLE	GRAPE VARIETIES
St-Joseph	Rhône, France	Red	Syrah
		White	Marsanne, Roussanne
Samos	Greece	White	Muscat Blanc à Petits Grains
Sancerre	Loire, France	White	Sauvignon Blanc
Saumur-Champigny	Loire, France	Red	Cabernet Franc, Cabernet Sauvignon, Pineau d'Aunis
		Rosé	Cabernet Franc, Cabernet Sauvignon, Pineau d'Aunis, Gamay, Cot, Groslot
		White	Chenin Blanc, Chardonnay, Sauvignon Blanc
Sauternes	Bordeaux, France	Sweet white	Sémillon, Sauvignon Blanc, Muscadelle
Savennières	Loire, France	White	Chenin Blanc
Savigny-Les-Beaune	Burgundy, France	Red	Pinot Noir
		White	Chardonnay
Soave	Veneto, Italy	White	Garganega, Pinot Bianco, Chardonnay, Trebbiano
St-Estèphe	Bordeaux, France	Red	Cabernet Sauvignon, Merlot, Cabernet Franc, Malbec, Petit Verdot
St-Julien	Bordeaux, France	Red	Cabernet Sauvignon, Merlot, Cabernet Franc, Malbec, Petit Verdot
St-Véran	Burgundy, France	White	Chardonnay
Tavel	Rhône, France	Rosé	Grenache Noir, Cinsault, Clairette Blanche, Clairette Picpoul, Calitor, Syrah, Carignan
Tokàji	Hungary	White	Furmint, Harslevelu
Vacqueyras	Rhône, France	Red	Grenache Noir, Syrah, Mourvèdre
		Rosé	Grenache Noir, Mourvèdre, Cinsault
		White	Grenache Blanc, Clairette Blanc, Bourboulenc, Marsanne Blanc, Roussanne Blanc, Viognier
Valdepeñas	Spain	Red	Cencibel
		White	Airén
Valpolicella	Veneto, Italy	Red	Corvina Veronese, Rondinella, Molinara

NAME	REGION/ COUNTRY	COLOR/ STYLE	GRAPE VARIETIES
Vin de Corse	Corsica, France	Red/rosé	Nielluccio, Sciacarello, Grenache, Cinsault, Mourvèdre ++
		White	Vermentino, Ugni Blanc
Vin Jaune (Côtes du Jura)	Jura, France	Sweet white	Sauvignon Blanc
Vesuvio	Campania, Italy	Red	Piedirosso, Sciascinoso
		White	Coda di Volpe, Verdeca
Vinho Verde	Portugal	Red	Vinhao, Espadeiro, Azal Tinto, Borraçal, Brancelho, Pedral
		White	Loureiro, Trajadura, Paderna, Azal, Avesso, Alvarinho
Vino Nobile de Montepulciano	Tuscany, Italy	Red	Sangiovese, Canaiolo Nero
Volnay	Burgundy, France	Red	Pinot Noir
Vosne-Romanée	Burgundy, France	Red	Pinot Noir
Vouvray	Loire, France	Dry/sweet white	Chenin Blanc
Zitsa	Greece	White	Debina

MAJOR INFLUENCES ON THE TASTE OF WINE

You have already seen that there are a number of influences on the taste of a particular wine, and I have talked about the taste of wine in the context of its grape variety. In the descriptions of the grape varieties, I have referred to climate, soil, yields, and winemaking techniques. These all have direct influences on the grape's taste. Let's find out exactly how.

How Does Soil Type Affect a Wine's Taste?

Soil is defined by its richness in fertilizing elements (which affects the plant's vigor); its structure (whether it is compact, rocky, or muddy); its mineral composition (granite, chalk, or limestone); its color (red soils warm up faster in springtime than lighter-colored soils); and its topographical situation (on a hill, in a valley, or on a plain).

Soil—in combination with its exposure to the sun and other climatic elements—creates *terroir,* essentially the French word for dirt! *Terroir* is not a place but a happening, a combination of circumstances. *Terroir* defies description and cannot be reproduced or fabricated. Either it happens or it doesn't, and either a place has it or it doesn't. And a *terroir* can be wasted if the right grape variety is not married to it. Furthermore, designating a particular parcel of soil as an appellation does not automatically bestow upon it the title of *terroir.* Clearly, *terroir* affects the taste of the wine to a considerable degree; it is, in fact, probably the major difference between a good wine and a great one.

Different grape varieties prefer certain soil types to others, and there is a good reason why some grapes match some soils better. Vines need soils that will store moisture reserves for droughts, drain excess water during heavy rains, and force the vine to grow deep roots to search for its nourishment, thereby developing character and strength. Vines on hillsides are going to need different soils from vines planted in valleys, which are vulnerable to stagnation and poor-draining pockets, thereby producing diluted, diseased fruit. As James Wilson, author of the book *Terroir,* so eloquently explains: "Vine roots are predatory in their search for lenses of fine-grained material and pounce on them ravenously. Roots are almost human in their perseverance to penetrate the barren layers and hardpan, passing through them without branching, in search of nourishing lenses. The characteristics of the vine must therefore complement the characteristics of the soil on which it is cultivated, and the balance between the variables is a delicate one."

For example, Syrah wines from the Rhône Valley's top *terroir,* Les Bessards (which has an entirely granite soil), in the same year, in the same vineyard, of the same estate, will have a leathery and spicy smell on the nose and the mouth will be very tannic. These wines will age very well. On the other hand, the same grapes from Meal (a *terroir* of stony soils on hills and terraces) have very fruity and delicate aromas, and an elegant mouth with nice round tannins.

Take Bordeaux. In an oversimplification, the various proportions of grape varieties used in the blends are based on how suited each of the varieties are to the *terroir* in question. St-Emilion wines are a majority of Merlot, then Cabernet Franc, with Cabernet Sauvignon and Malbec in smaller doses because St-Emilion's soils welcome the Merlot more than the soils of, say, Pauillac or Pomerol, which are Cabernet Sauvignon–dominated plantings.

Another example is the Gamay grape. Philip the Bold was right. In the granite terrain of Beaujolais with its thin, sandy soils, it produces a fine and agreeable wine—though when planted on the rich limestone soils found just a few miles toward the north on the Côte d'Or, the variety produces a wine that is light, thin, and not very pleasant. Closer to home, you need only taste the differences between a Zinfandel from San Luis Obispo below Monterey or the Sierra foothills and one from Amador County to understand. This observation can be made with other varieties and other *terroirs*. The only conclusion is clear: Each variety has a soil that best expresses its originality.

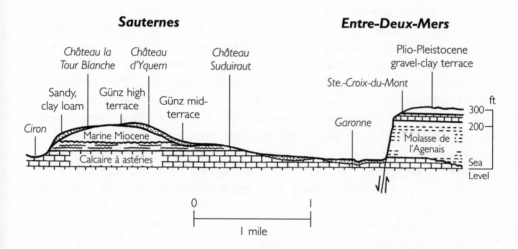

The story of soil: A geological slice of Bordeaux's soil composition. (Adapted from *Terroir* by James E. Wilson, Mitchell-Beazley, 1998.)

How Does Climate Affect a Wine's Taste?

A grape needs to mature on a vine before it is picked. If the weather is too cold, the grapes will not mature and will thus taste green and acidic. If it is too hot, they will reach maturity too quickly—but it will be a superficial maturity and not complete. White wines from a hot climate will lack acidity and therefore taste flabby and too sweet, while red wines will have too much alcohol and will have a very forward "first attack" before seeming to evaporate on the tongue, and completely disappearing before they get down your throat. The correct climate is needed to ensure that the growing period, or the ripening period, is long and slow.

Furthermore, the warmer and sunnier the climate, the less distinction there will be between grape varieties and the less the varietal character will develop. This is because in cool-climate areas, the lesser amounts of sunshine produce high levels of odor-active compounds. Higher levels are produced because the cooler weather permits a longer, slower fruit maturation. You can smell these compounds (aromatic esters and aldehydes) as the familiar primary aromas of a grape variety. This is why climates that are too warm are really not conducive to quality grape growing. There will also be less variation from year to year, and vintage will therefore be less of an issue.

Believe it or not, with a trained palate, you can detect the climatic origin of a wine. You can taste whether it came from a hot climate or a cool one—they taste quite different. You have probably tasted the difference yourself before but may or may not have realized what was making this difference. To put it simply, wines from a hotter climate will taste almost cooked or boiled, whereas wines from a cooler climate will taste fresher and cooler. Why?

For each grape variety there is a specific climatic area where it best expresses its quality potential. For example, Riesling is perfectly adapted to the continental climate of Alsace, and the Pinot Noir to the continental climate of Burgundy. The Syrah is used to a temperate climate like that of the Rhône Valley, the Mourvèdre to a southern climate, and the Cabernet Sauvignon to the oceanic climate of the Bordeaux region. This is why there is such a difference between the way grape varieties taste in different countries. Chardonnay in Chablis is crisp and acidic, whereas in the Napa Valley it tastes oaky and tropical.

If a variety meant for a warm climate is grown in a cooler climate, its character is refined. For example, if the Grenache, of Spanish origin, is planted in the Côtes du Rhône, it produces finer, more delicate wines. And the inverse is true. If a variety is planted in a more southerly climate than its original home, then it will make a heavier wine, with heavier aromas and with a higher alcohol content. Winemakers sometimes add acidity to a flabby wine grown in a too-warm location rather than take the risk of planting a variety in a place where it may not ripen every year.

Sunlight permits and encourages the accumulation of sugars, but not sunlight alone. It cannot get the job done unless it is accompanied by the right temperatures—and, more important, the sum of temperatures throughout the growing period of the vine. This is what people are referring to when they talk about "growing days" or "heat summation." The general rule is that the warmer it is during the period directly preceding the harvesting of the grapes, the higher the sugar levels will be, and the lower the acidity. Inversely, the cooler the temperatures at this time, the lower the grape's sugar content will be, and the richer its acidity levels.

The synthesis of the polyphenols (coloring agents) is also in direct relation to the temperature. The warmer it is during the period just before harvesttime, the more color and tannins the red grapes will have when harvested.

The relationship among the sugar, acid, and polyphenols is a crucial one and is additionally influenced by the precipitation the vines receive during the maturation period. The best balance among them is achieved when the vines have a humid vegetative cycle (but not too wet) until the *veraison* (when the grape ripens from green to white or red-black) to permit optimum growth, then a rather dry period just before harvesting so the sugars reach their optimum levels.

For each type of climate there is a corresponding type of wine, the character of which will be defined by the balance of alcohol/acid and tannin.

Grapes grown in a warm and dry climate, such as the Mediterranean, will produce a wine that is rich in sugars and has relatively few acids, but is rich in polyphenols. An oceanic climate has fairly even temperatures with average sunshine, and produces grapes that have average sugar and acid levels but are rather rich in polyphenols. A continental climate is one that produces grapes average in sugars, relatively acidic, and lacking a bit in polyphenols.

The majority of the world's vineyards are in areas that enjoy a Mediterranean climate, such as Italy, Greece, Spain, Portugal, North Africa, Asia, South Africa, Australia, California, and Chile. In this type of climate, the white wines won't have very much aroma and will lack acidity. To fix this, winemakers use technological advances such as fermenting at low temperatures and blocking the malolactic fermentation to obtain a fresh and aromatic white wine. This is fine, but you must be conscious of the fact that white wines of great quality should reflect and be typical of not only their vinification method but also their climate, soil, and grape variety. In other words, yes, we can fix things, but in doing so we've changed them and inevitably altered their quality.

How Does Yield Affect Wine's Taste?

One of the first issues that will greatly affect a wine's quality and taste can be influenced even before the grapes get into the winery. This is the vineyard's yields, or the volume of grapes the vineyard is allowed to grow. Every year, the minimum and maximum yields are fixed in the various appellations of Europe, depending upon weather and crop conditions.

Very much like rosebushes or other plants in our gardens, grapevines need to be treated in such a way that they do not go wild. A plant that is overnourished will actually produce more foliage than fruit. Too much of either leaves or fruit is bad. For every grape variety, an augmentation of yields will dilute all its characteristics: color, sugar, acids, and tannins. Inversely, small yields will best show off the grape's character. The variation of yields depends upon several things: whether or not a prolific rootstock was chosen, the planting density of the vines, their fertilization and watering program, and the pruning techniques employed.

Planting Density

As we have seen, both too many clusters on a branch and too many branches on a vine allow a plant to produce too much fruit. However, another factor to consider is the number of plants, or vines, allowed to grow in any one area, such as a hectare of vines. The French call this the *pieds de vignes,* or the "feet of vines," planted. Vines that are planted very close together will have to fight for survival. They will have to struggle and compete with each other for the nutrients and water in the soil. Thus their roots will be forced to run deeper into the ground, unlike plants that are planted far apart, the roots of which tend to spread out horizontally and superficially and thus become lazy, as all they need is easily accessible to them. So, like a spoiled child, they will lack character. Stressing vines, whether by planting them closer together on hillsides or by heavy pruning, builds character and therefore allows a higher level of quality.

Why are plants sometimes planted farther apart? For monetary reasons, usually. Fewer plants planted means less cost in terms of buying the plants and tending the parcel. Also, when plants are close together, machine harvesters cannot fit between the rows to pick the fruit—it has to be done by hand. This means hand laborers, which is slower and more expensive.

It is also interesting to note that planting density is, or should be, tied to climate. In cooler climates, the density is traditionally about twenty to twenty-five thousand plants per acre, while in warmer climates, ten to twelve thousand is more the norm. Any less than this and the quality can be compromised. So to obtain richer grapes, it is best to permit as few clusters as possible on the plant, which is achieved by planting the plants very close together. Before the phylloxera crisis—when the fungal infection spread like wildfire through the vineyards and decimated many wine-producing areas—there were some plantings in Champagne and Burgundy that were as dense as forty-nine thousand plants per acre!

Pruning

If a vine were not pruned, it would develop terrifically during the first few years, exhausting its growth and shortening its life. It would bear fewer grapes, and the quality of these grapes would not be as good. It is necessary to control the growth of a young vine in proportion to its strength and the depth of its root system, therefore pruning is individual to every vine. Pruning can be performed at two stages during the year: in December or January after the harvest when the vines are in hibernation, and in July or August—called green pruning, because the vines are in their vegetative cycle.

The Age of the Plants

Another factor affecting yields is the age of the vines. Older vines that have been well pruned and not squeezed to maximum production will slowly yield fewer, more concentrated grapes as they get older. Vines are just getting interesting when they hit thirty years or more. So it is best if they arrive at that ripe age in a sober fashion. Vines that *pissent*—a very elegant French term for being overworked—are drained and worn out by the time they are twenty.

Even the age at which a winemaker allows a plant to start producing fruit is an important factor in a wine's overall taste and quality. On average, a new plant is pruned very severely and not allowed to produce any fruit until it is three or four years old. At either end of the spectrum, there are extremes. Those winemakers who are very commercially driven will sometimes let two-year-old plants produce fruit, and lots of it, while I know of a young winemaker who runs a family business in Germany who won't let the plants produce one grape until they are seven years old! Which would make the better wine in your opinion?

Determining Yield

So when determining yield, it is not enough to ask how many gallons per acre have been produced; other questions are equally important. How much pruning was done and how often? Are heavy fertilizers used? Is irrigation allowed? Which rootstock was chosen? How many plants per acre are there? How old are the plants? When were they first allowed to produce fruit? And so forth. These are all variables in the final equation of quantity and therefore quality.

How Does the Winemaking Technique Affect the Wine's Taste?

Having looked at the magic trilogy of soil, climate, and grape variety, there are those who would say there is a fourth element that is even more important (I wouldn't). Is that person a magician who makes it all possible, whose gentle hand leads the juice on the path of a greater beverage—or are the winemakers the ultimate intruders, manipulators who permanently imprint their personal style and interpretation of the grape onto each bottle? The answers are all of the above. It depends on the winemaker's politics and methodology.

Some winemakers claim that they are simply standing back and letting the fruit express itself, although meanwhile, they maximize the extraction of color and flavor when fermenting. Others might say they prefer to allow the soil to speak for itself and opt for winemaking methods that are more hands off.

These two different philosophies can be illustrated rather well in Burgundy. It is interesting to take a particular domain and try to determine whether each of its wines from different villages or vineyards reflect its variety and where it's grown, or if the common denominator of each wine is the style in which it has been made. I have tested this. I studied in great detail a particular winemaking family that has parcels in four or five of the well-known appellations in Burgundy. Up and down Burgundy, in all the blind tastings, you could actually pick out their wines—the style of the wine was definitely stamped with their technique rather than with the different wine parcels. You could barely tell the difference between the Pommard, the Volnay, and the Mercurey! All their wines were delicious, mind you, and the wine style was very elegant, but it became boring and completely counteracted the beauty and the point of Burgundy.

Another aspect of winemaking, and a rather modern one, is the advent of the flying winemaker. These are freelance winemakers who make wine for any number of clients anywhere in the world. Again, there are bad and good things in this. The original idea was supposed to have had something to do with spreading and communicating badly needed viticultural information to certain wine regions. Frenchmen were flying to Australia and California, Australians to Portugal, all of them to Hungary and Bulgaria. Top flying winemakers have become celebrities in the wine world. They have up to a couple of dozen clients around the globe. But at what point do information and knowledge stop being shared and personal style preferences take hold, creating homogeneity?

 ## WHEN TO PICK A GRAPE AND HOW THIS AFFECTS ITS TASTE

Just as each grape variety has a specific taste and aroma potential, it also has a window of time in which it has reached its maturity and should be picked. This is very important and is probably the hardest task a winemaker has, for nature doesn't always keep to schedule.

To put it simply, there are grapes that mature in the first period, those that mature in the second, and those in the third. Within those three categories, there are also grapes that are more precocious than others. So there exists a harvesting order corresponding to the time each grape variety matures. If a winemaker has a vineyard of Chardonnay (first), Cabernet Sauvignon (second), and Grenache (third), the grapes are brought in, or picked, in that order. Further, if the vineyard has Merlot (early second period), Cabernet Franc (middle to late second period), and Cabernet Sauvignon (late second period) plantings, then although they are all classed as second-period varieties, they will be harvested in that order because they mature in that order.

This order is for the noble European grape varieties and their native climate. Take a grape out of its native environment and a little jiggery-pokery has to go on. For example, the Chardonnay is a late-first-period, or *première epoque tardive,* grape. When grown in a warmer climate, it often reaches overmaturation (and so would taste flabby and too sweet) because it is so warm. The grower is therefore obliged to pick the grapes earlier, sometimes even before they are mature. To go ahead and vinify this type of grape will not give it a chance to express itself fully. The resulting taste will be one dimensional, overtly fruity, and short on the finish.

The chart below lists the major grape varieties and their comparative maturation periods in France. It is not exhaustive, but it provides an interesting comparison and should give you some insight into the correlation among climate, maturity, and taste. Notice that those grape varieties that appear to mature early, in the first period, are found in the northern or cooler climates of France. Those that mature somewhere in the second period are found in the more central climates, and those that are late maturing are in the south, where the climate is Mediterranean.

PERIOD OF MATURITY	GRAPE VARIETY	REGION OF FRANCE
First period	Gewürztraminer	Northeast
	Pinot Noir	
	Pinot Meunier	
	Gamay	
	Chardonnay	
	Sylvaner	
Second period	Sauvignon Blanc	West and southwest
	Colombard	Southwest
	Chenin Blanc	West

PERIOD OF MATURITY	GRAPE VARIETY	REGION OF FRANCE
	Viognier	Southeast
	Sémillon	Southwest
	Marsanne	Southeast
	Roussanne	Southeast
	Syrah	Southeast
	Cinsault	Southeast
	Merlot	Southwest
	Cabernet Franc	Southwest
	Cabernet Sauvignon	Southwest
Third period	Clairette	Mediterranean
	Ugni Blanc	
	Grenache	
	Carignan	
	Mourvèdre	

Choices for the Winemaker

There are many choices a winemaker has to make—and they will *all* affect the final taste of the wine.

Hand or Machine Harvesting?

If handpicked, the grapes will arrive at the winery in better condition. Those that are ripest, least bruised, and healthy will be distinguished from those that are unripe, bruised, and rotten. Also, any unwanted debris can be avoided. This means a cleaner wine, less vulnerable later to unwanted flavors. However, handpicking is labor intensive and therefore very expensive. Most of the traditional vineyards continue this practice, while modern ones plant their vines farther apart on purpose so that harvesting machines can fit between the rows and do the picking. Despite any hand sorting later in the winery, this means more bruised grapes and debris.

To Partially or Fully Separate Stems and Stalks?

Before maceration and fermentation, the winemaker has to decide how much, if any, of the stalks is going to be separated from the grapes. If they are allowed to remain in contact with the must (the unfermented grape juice) and the must is rather delicate or light (due to either the grape variety, the style of wine, or dilution caused by rain), then they can turn the wine sour and astringent. The wine could even taste of sticks and branches. If the must has the strength to take it (an intense red variety in a good year), then leaving some stalks and stems in with the rest of the grape can give it more structure, as these parts of the grape contain tannins, acids, and some minerals.

How Long to Macerate the Wine

The length of time the skins remain in contact with must is only relevant when making red wines. This is what gives the must its color, flavor, and structure. A long maceration is used for the noble grape varieties such as Cabernet Sauvignon, Pinot Noir, Nebbiolo, and Syrah because they have better-quality skins. Other red grape varieties will need less time in the vat. If they are macerated for too long, the skin extracts will make the wine taste bitter, green, and hard.

How to Start and at What Temperature to Ferment the Must

The first fermentation that grape juice undergoes is the alcoholic fermentation. This is simply allowing the yeasts to convert the juice's sugars to alcohol. The only problem is that sometimes the yeasts do not get going on their own and need a jump start. Ideally, a winemaker can use indigenous yeasts from that vineyard, but if for some reason this is not possible, a winemaker can purchase commercial yeasts and use them to initiate fermentation. Yeasts of this sort can be bought in different flavors, such as apricot, banana, or peach, in order to give an otherwise light raw material more appeal. So sometimes, this is what you taste!

Assuming things get off naturally, red wines are allowed to ferment at a higher temperature than whites to extract more color and flavor. But beware. If allowed to ferment at too high a temperature, the yeasts will become inactive and the fermentation will come to a halt, or the wine will taste cooked or boiled.

Whether to Allow a Partial or Full Malolactic Fermentation

This is the second fermentation, and is when the malic acids (which taste like green apples) are transformed into lactic acids (which taste like yogurt), making the wine more supple. It is usually only applied to white wines, as they can be more acidic. A winemaker can allow a partial or full malolactic fermentation, and this greatly alters a wine's taste. As a matter of fact, you can usually tell if the wine has undergone such a fermentation or not. Typically, a wine from a cool climate, like Champagne or Alsace, might need a partial or full fermentation to soften some of the acids without losing their crisp, applelike tastes and smells. In wines made from grapes in a warmer climate, on the other hand, the winemaker might not let it occur, or the wine would be too flabby and sweet.

The Length of Barrel Aging and the Sort of Wood Program

After fermentation, the wine is usually put into containers of various sizes for aging. The container chosen is most often an oak barrel. Red wines, depending on their quality and structure, will usually be aged for anywhere between six months and two years. White wines are usually aged for less than six months, or not at all.

Of all the decisions a winemaker has to make about oak—whether to use it during fermentation, aging, or both; to use new oak, used oak, or both; how long to use it; whether to choose light, medium, or heavy toast—one of the most important (toasting is also crucial) will be the selection of its origins, but not for the reasons that most of us would assume. The question is not Alliers, Nevers, or Limousin (all French oak forests), and the argument should not be French versus American or even Slovenian, Hungarian, or Russian, for there are variations in quality and confusion of hybrids in all these places. The primary factor in the selection of oak quality is tight grain versus wide grain, and only secondly how much is used; too much of even the best oak is too much.

Even oak trees have their problems of soil, site, and climate, and forests in cooler climates produce trees that have tight grains. This permits a more subtle transfer of vanillin and less extraction of the aggressive oak flavors.

Overoaking is a big problem in modern winemaking. It started with the late-1970s California trend of showing off your new, expensive, imported French oak barrels. But today, there is still the even worse offense of hoping that the oak barrels will provide the tannins, flavor, and complexity that the fruit is lacking. The problem is often not that there is too much oak, but that there is not enough good fruit. When used as the key ingredient, oak can mask many faults and deficiencies. Oak should be the spice of the recipe, not the flour!

Competent winemakers will evaluate the structure of the wine and decide how much oak it can take. They may put only one-third of the wine in new oak, one-third in two-year-old oak, and the last third in stainless steel. This is what is referred to as a wood program, and again, it is all about balance and getting the best recipe to fit the raw material. Red wine that has spent too long in new oak will taste dry and harsh, while white wine that has spent too long in new oak often ends up tasting bitter and resiny.

What Effect Does Aging Have on Wine?

It is a known fact that a wine is a living entity that improves with age and changes with its evolution—that is, if it is made from a grape variety that is physiologically intended to improve with age, if this grape variety is grown in the most suitable climate, and if the appropriate winemaking techniques have been applied. If that is the case, there will be a definite difference between what's known as the primary aromas of a wine, or its grape variety while young, and the more developed smells that come from oak and bottle aging—what's called the wine's bouquet.

What Is Maturation?

Assuming that everything goes all right until bottling, wine will continue to mature. In very simple terms, the maturation of a wine is the function of its composition, its origin *(terroir),* and its vintage. No two bottles from the same Bordeaux château, of two different years, will develop and mature in the same number of years.

When you let a wine mature, you are waiting for all its components to fall into balance with each other. A good wine is one that is balanced and harmonious. The acids, alcohols, tannins, and fruits have all blended into one, creating a personality, a character. A less good wine will never fall into place, because the fruits will die; or the tannins will fade away into nothing instead of softening and holding the wine together; or the acids, the backbone and life of the wine, may become flabby or disappear. When tasting a young wine, look for all of these elements and try to determine how well the wine is made and how it will mature. You can be rather certain of a wine's character, but you never really know whether that character will endure until you test it years later.

During bottle aging, red wines deposit little plaques and grains of coloring agents and other molecules, which bond and fall to the bottom of the bottle. The heavier clusters settle faster than the smaller ones, which need years to settle. As these coloring agents settle in the bottles, the intensity of the wine's color diminishes, becoming more and more reddish brick and finally yellowish as the anthocyanins, or coloring agents, in the tannins soften and diminish while the tannins do. When I say that the tannins soften, I mean that the wine has reached a point of balance in its development curve. The harsh edge is taken off and the wine's texture is smoother and less drying.

Polymerization progresses continually as the wine ages, so that tannic wines for long aging become gradually harder and more tannic before reaching a peak where they are more tannic than when they were in the barrel. Then the slope starts a gradual decline. The extra-large molecules lose their ability to combine with other proteins, and their astringency diminishes. At the same time, they are combining with other components in the wine, becoming insoluble and precipitating to form the characteristic deposit. At this point the wine is in its mature, mellow phase and is softer, richer, and rounder: This is maturity.

If kept too long, the increasingly large polymers gather strength once more, a sort of final wind, and become dry and astringent once again. This is compounded by the fact that the wine is also losing its fruit and gaining volatile acidity. It is drying out, or dying. Knowing at which moment to open a wine is a skill acquired, happily, through much practice!

Certain wines will reach maturity sooner than others, and not every wine will have the same length of maturity. In general, the duration of a wine's ideal maturation period is the length it needed to reach it. If a 1990 Latour will reach its apogee in 2010, then you can hope to be able to enjoy your bottles for twenty years.

What Does a Mature Wine Taste Like?

To best describe how a mature wine tastes, imagine the following analogies:

YOUNG	MATURE
Fresh cherries	Black cherry jam
Citrus fruit	Tropical fruit
Fresh red fruit	Cooked, warm red fruit
Fresh fig	Dried fig
Green pepper	Black pepper
Honeysuckle	Honey or caramel
Green apples	Apple crumble
Orange juice	Orange liqueur
Peanuts	Roasted almonds
Freshly cut grass	Wet straw or hay
Cinnamon gum	Mulled wine

Does this give you an idea? Proper aging adds depth and complexity to an odor. Plus there are some odors that are not even apparent in a wine until some oak aging or bottle aging has taken place, such as cigar and tobacco smells and those of mushrooms and undergrowth. There is no "young" smell analogy for these.

HOW TO TASTE WINE

Many techniques have been developed by wine professionals to help you to maximize the taste experience.

When you taste a wine you are looking out for many things, because whether or not you like the wine will depend on many factors. You are tasting for balance among the acids, tannins, alcohol, and fruit—acids for the backbone, tannins for preservation and longevity, alcohol for its structure, and fruit for its taste. The better a wine is made, the more balanced it will be, and the longer it will last.

Tasting a wine is merely breaking down the different components of taste and analyzing them. Anyone can do it, but it does take concentration and practice. The more you taste, the more memory you will have, and the more information you will collect with which to create your own standards. As your skill increases, you will be able to blind-taste the difference between a red and white wine, recognize a Cabernet Sauvignon grape or a Pinot Noir, know whether the wine is from France, the United States, or Australia, determine if a wine was made in a hot or cool climate, and be able to tell a young wine from an older one.

The process of tasting a wine is basically broken into three categories: sight, smell, and taste. Fill the glass no more than one-third full when tasting and never more than half full at the table.

Sight

With the glass held vertically, look down on it from directly above. This will allow you to view the wine's surface, clearness, depth of color, and any carbon dioxide (bubbles) that may be present.

With the glass tilted almost in a horizontal position against a white tablecloth, look at the wine (red) at its center as well as its rim. The center, or eye, of the wine will determine its hue and help you know its age. The lighter, or rubier, red a red wine is, the younger it is. Once it is in the red-brick or orange tones, you know it is older. By looking at its rim, you can also determine its age. The younger the wine, the thinner the watery rim will be; the older the wine, the thicker this watery rim will be.

Now look at the wine horizontally, with your eyes directly at its disk level. This enables you to observe the wine's robe, or color, which, as described above, will help you determine the wine's age. With white wines, the color will tell you a lot about its weight and taste intensity. A very light, watery color will almost always mean a light, watery wine. You will also be looking for deposits. In an older red, this would be normal; even if decanted well there may be bits that escaped. With whites, deposits used to mean a wine had good extracts; they were considered perfectly natural and desirable. However, in today's world, most people prefer wines to be as stable and (in my opinion) sterile as possible so as to better survive the conditions imposed by international transport and storage. Some people get a bit squeamish if there are bits of pulp or fining material in their Pouilly-Fuissé!

Next, tilt the glass so a little wine covers the sides. Look at it again horizontally at eye level, but look for the little tears or legs running down the side of the glass. Are they slow and languorous or thin and rapid? The slower the legs run, the more glucose (sugar) is present in the wine, and the more watery or fast the legs run, the more alcohol is present in the wine. This will already give you a first idea of how the wine may taste.

Smell

Before swirling, smell the wine. This will permit you to smell any varietal qualities or characteristics.

Then swirl the glass and smell again. Use either one or both nostrils. It sounds odd, but experiment with each nostril; you might be surprised at the differences. You should be looking for major faults and remarking the differences from when the wine was still. Here you'll find more intense aromas for young wines and a bouquet for mature wines.

If you think you've detected a fault, or if you can't seem to wake up the wine's nose, continue swirling or cover the glass and shake it violently once or twice.

CAN YOU TASTE WINE FAULTS?

Improper harvesting and production techniques, handling, and storage can all cause wine faults. Here are a few you might discover when tasting wine.

WHAT IT TASTES LIKE	WHAT HAPPENED	WHEN IT HAPPENED
Rot and a bitter herbaceousness like crushed green leaves	The grapes were damaged by hail or were rotten, or there were leaves and other foreign objects with the grapes.	During harvest
Herbaceous (in excess)	The grapes were roughly treated and poorly destemmed, destalked, and crushed, or the grapes were immature at harvest.	Arrival at winery

WHAT IT TASTES LIKE	WHAT HAPPENED	WHEN IT HAPPENED
Bitter; stalks, stems, and branches	The grapes were pressed too violently, which bruises the skin.	Pressing of white grapes
Dry, sour, and astringent tannins	The *cuvaison* (vatting time) was too long.	Fermentation
Thin and light	The *cuvaison* was too short.	Fermentation
Taste of cooked caramel	The temperature was too high.	Fermentation
Lacks color and structure	The temperature was too low.	Fermentation
Earthy, manure-type smells	Brettanomyces (brett), a strain of yeast, is liked by some but disliked by many Californians. In small amounts it adds character; in large amounts it is considered offensive.	Fermentation
Flavor of fresh dirt or cement	Dekkera is another wild yeast of the genus brett. Liked by some in France, it can also come from contaminated equipment and barrels.	Fermentation
Taste of the lees	There was no racking or not enough.	Racking
Taste of oxidation (flat and aldehydic)	There was too much racking.	Racking
Tastes oxidized, musty, stale, and dirty	The container was opened and reclosed.	*Elevage*
Tastes of a moldy *cuve* or tank	The container is dirty or moldy.	*Elevage*
Smell of rotten eggs	Too much hydrogen sulfide from bacterial contamination. Can sometimes be cured by airing.	*Elevage*

WHAT IT TASTES LIKE	WHAT HAPPENED	WHEN IT HAPPENED
Smell of burnt matches	Too much sulfur dioxide was used. Can sometimes be cured by airing.	Preparation and cleaning of oak barrels
Taste of sulfur	Too much sulfur was used.	Preparation for bottling and bottling
Heavy deposits	Poor filtering.	Preparation for bottling and bottling
Taste of rotten cork	Bad cork.	Preparation for bottling and bottling
Smells like musty cardboard or a damp basement	The wine is corked. This is caused by trichloranisol (TCA), a compound released by molds that can infest the bark from which corks are made. One theory is that you cannot get TCA without chlorine, which is used to bleach corks, so if corks aren't properly rinsed and dried after bleaching, this problem can occur.	Preparation for bottling and bottling
No fruit flavor left, off color	Wine is madeirized, or subjected to oxygen or heat through poor storage. It ends up tasting like Madeira or Sherry.	Storage
Sharp, tart, green, thin, like an unripe grape	Excessive acidity, excessive fixed or volatile acidity, a high proportion of tannins, or too much ethyl acetate.	Fermentation

WHAT IT TASTES LIKE	WHAT HAPPENED	WHEN IT HAPPENED
Smell of rotten eggs, garlic, onion, or even skunk	Reduction of a wine results in a smell of mercaptans, which are formed by yeast reacting with sulfur in the lees.	During primary alcoholic fermentation
Vinegar smell	Volatile acidity. This indicates the presence of acetic acid caused by bacteria. Airing can help.	Fermentation

Taste

Some people advise taking a small sip, but I tend to take large mouthfuls of wine, which helps me feel or "chew" the wine's texture more easily. Or I take a small first sip, go through my analysis, and then take a second, much larger, sip and rinse it through my mouth like mouthwash to either confirm or discount my first impressions. It's up to you to decide what works best. This first taste is meant to judge the *première bouche* or "first attack." Is it soft or firm, smooth or sharp? How soon afterward do you feel the tannins, the acids, the texture?

Swish the wine around in your mouth. Go ahead and make that gurgling, airy noise between your teeth to aerate the wine. Swallow a tiny bit. Concentrate on what is happening on your tongue and on the sides of your mouth. Are you experiencing a puckering, drying sensation? Young, tannic wines will do this. Is it velvety smooth, with softened tannins indicating an older wine that is correctly aged? Is it like butter, all creamy and almost thick? This is where the "mouth" is determined. Is it ample or thin? Here you can also fully analyze the wine's flavors, its intensity, and its texture.

Spit the wine, breathe out through your nose and palate, and concentrate on the back of your mouth. Here you analyze the finale, or finish, of the wine. The better the wine, the longer it will linger in the back of your palate. Here also the balance of the tastes and aromas is important. A wine that has a delicious up-front, fruity attack and an ample, warm mouth often disappoints once it gets to the finish. An overly alcoholic wine with lots of heavy fruit, spice, and oak flavors up front will fool you until the finish, where it is short or even nonexistent, a certain sign that the wine is unbalanced. Even an immature wine will show some signs of the shape of its future; and a complete lack of finish, at any stage, is a bad one.

HOW DOES THE WINE'S TEMPERATURE AFFECT ITS TASTE?

If ever you are served a wine, either red, rosé, or white, that is really chilled, be wary. When a wine is super cold, you can no longer taste it, and therefore any attributes or faults it may have are masked. Often inexpensive rosés or Primeur reds are served like this for that very reason! And drinking wines that are too warm has the opposite effect. Every aspect of the wine is laid bare before you and to its worst advantage. And beware: Contrary to popular belief, room temperature can often be too hot.

Last summer, I ordered a bottle of red Burgundy in a restaurant, and because I had noticed that the wine rack was directly over the hot, vibrating stereo system next to the kitchen door, I asked for an ice bucket. The waitress looked a bit confused, went away, and then came back to the table, smugly announcing that the Burgundy I ordered was indeed "a red wine, madam, and is served at room temperature." I replied, even more smugly, that room temperature in that particular room, at that particular moment, was near, or over, seventy-seven degrees Fahrenheit and the Burgundy I had ordered was meant to be enjoyed at fifty-nine to sixty-three degrees. So could she please bring an ice bucket? She didn't look convinced, but grudgingly complied. This happens to me all the time. And I am not particularly fond of boiled Pinot Noir.

Remember that the word *chambré* in French is the adjective form of *chambre*, or room. When château walls were feet thick and there was no central heating, room temperature was between sixty-one and sixty-four degrees at most (if they were lucky!). Serving a red at sixty-eight to seventy-seven degrees often alters the taste of the wine. When serving a red wine that has not come from the cellar and is warm, you should not refer to this as chilling the wine—because you are not, you are simply bringing it back to the temperature at which it should be served. A red wine served too warm is too heavy, alcoholic, and flat tasting. At the correct temperature it will be lively and more flavorful—too cold and it will have no taste at all.

Serving Temperatures

Sparkling wines

Simple sparkling (Cava, Crémant, Saumur, nonvintage Champagne)	5–7°C/41–45°F
Sweet sparkling	4–7°C/39–45°F
Finest sparkling and vintage Champagne	6–9°C/43–48°F

White wines
Simple, sweet whites (Anjou Blanc, Muscat,
German QbA)   4–8°C/39–46°F

Simple, crisp, dry whites (Muscadet, Sancerre,
Sauvignon Blanc, Pinot Blanc)   6–8°C/43–46°F

Complex dry whites (Burgundy, Graves, Rioja)   9–11°C/48–52°F

Medium sweet whites (German Spätlese, Auslese,
New World Riesling)   10–12°C/50–54°F

Finest sweet whites (classed-growth Sauternes,
top German wine, late-harvest wine)   5–9°C/41–48°F

Finest dry whites (mature white Burgundy,
Graves, top New World Chardonnay)   10–12°C/50–54°F

Rosé wines (simplest should be most chilled)   6–8°C/43–46°F

Red wines
Early-drinking reds (Loire, simple Beaujolais,
Côtes du Rhône, *vins de pays*)   10–12°C/50–54°F

Simple reds (young Bordeaux and Burgundies,
New World reds)   14–15°C/57–59°F

Complex, mature reds, notably Pinot Noirs
(Burgundy, New World Pinot Noir, Italian and
Spanish reds)   16–17°C/61–63°F

Mature fine reds, notably Cabernet Sauvignons
(classed-growth Bordeaux, serious New World
Cabernets, Côtes du Rhône)   17–18°C/63–64°F

Fortified wines
Dry (Fino Sherry)   9–11°C/48–52°F

Medium (Amontillado Sherry, Madeira, white Port)   10–12°C/50–54°F

Sweet (cream Sherry, tawny Port, vintage Port)   15–16°C/59–61°F

Getting It All Together

These are just some of the decisions that affect the final product—the wine
you drink—but they give you a pretty good idea why wines taste as they do.
And as all this information on wine has probably made you hungry, let's
move on to the taste of food.

PART 2

THE
TASTE
OF
FOOD

The first sign that I was to have a special relationship with food was at birth. My mother delights in recounting the fact that I was the first baby in the history of the hospital to finish my first bottle and ask for more. The affair continued well throughout my childhood and is marked by another memorable anecdote—my personal favorite. At the gustatorily naive age of twelve, our Girl Scout troop, of which my mother was the leader, embarked on a backpacking adventure near the Grand Canyon. This was to be a foray into the true wild. We were all outfitted with special backpacks, space blankets, and lightweight cooking gear. To top it off, my mother made a noble attempt to keep the trip authentically austere by spending a fortune on powdered food of the type used by astronauts. She very halfheartedly planned our daily menus entirely from a selection of aluminum foil packets.

But I would not have it. Carry a thirty-pound pack—yes; piddle in the middle of the woods with no toilet paper—yes; run the risk of meeting a coyote—yes; but eat powdered scrambled eggs—*no!* So as the rest of the troop was outside loading the Suburban, I quickly raided the kitchen, taking three eggs, bacon, a frozen sirloin steak, and a large potato with fresh butter and chives. Tucking these safely into my pack, I smugly set off with the rest of the girls.

I waited, sadistically, until we had suffered a day and a half of powdered meals. Then early one morning, as everyone was tucking into their corn-flakes in powdered milk, I buttered my miniature frying pan (also borrowed from my mother's pantry) and broke open the eggs. I threw on the bacon and sat back, sipping my hot tea, imagining the feast to come. The odor soon wafted over to my mother's tent and very soon a furry cap emerged. "I smell eggs, *real* eggs!" The next instant, the entire troop was sitting round my fire trying to figure out how to divide three eggs into fifteen portions. I left them to it, as they didn't know what I had up my sleeve for dinner that night! Needless to say, I didn't earn any badges on that trip.

FROM WINE TO FOOD

I'm now moving, in a sense, from one food group to another, because most of the principles I established in part 1 can be applied to food. You know a lot more about wine than you think you do, just by being a food lover. In fact, learning about wine is probably easier than learning about food, as there are even more variables affecting a dish's taste than there are for a wine.

The things that are important to a grape's quality—and therefore the quality of the wine—are the same things that we look for when choosing our food. We all prefer fresh food to stale, colorful to pale, tasty to bland, and purity of taste to ambiguity.

The only problem with today's food industry is that we cannot count on any of the home-grown ingredients that were taken for granted by all country dwellers until the 1940s. Unlike wine, we have no idea where our food comes from. There are no appellation restrictions for tomatoes or potatoes, for example; we know only that our eggs are "free range" or that our meat is prime or choice; and other than the rare farmer's markets, we have to rely on large supermarkets, which can ship in goods from anywhere in the world. So where good farming used to be directly responsible for good cooking and good eating, it seems that good shopping is the modern equivalent.

Nature has a reason for everything. Interestingly, the more I learn about food and wine, the more I find myself referring to gardening encyclopedias! I think that is the beauty of the industry. It marries so many disciplines: history, geography, chemistry, climatology, geology, ecology, and agriculture.

FOOD'S NATURAL INFLUENCES

The analogies between food and wine are endless. Food, like wine, needs to be grown in good soils with enough sunlight and rain, to be produced in small yields and with careful harvesting and preparation techniques. Just as there are different grape varieties, there are different varieties of tomato, of mushroom, of potato, of apple. Then, just like wine, each variety is further differentiated by its origins. The same things that provide a country or region with its variances in wine (the landscape, the vegetation, the soil, and the climate) are all things that lend a food its diversity. And just as there is a grape variety suited to a set of geographical conditions, so is there a geographical set of conditions ideal for a food item: Figs grow at their best in the Mediterranean, apples in the northern United States, salmon in Norway, butter in Normandy, truffles in the Perigord, goat's cheese in the Loire Valley, Parma ham and Parmesan cheese in Tuscany, and so on.

Even in blending, there are similarities between food and wine. Just as a fine Bordeaux is blended from the very best of a winemaker's *cuvées,* so is the fine, sweet, corn cereal, polenta. There are four types of polenta grain and an authentic way to make polenta. The finest producers strive for smaller yields to maintain quality. Then they mix the four grains each year according to their flavor and quality and to the secret recipe or blend of the individual producer. Doesn't that sound familiar?

THE MANIPULATION OF FOOD AND WINE

Cooking methods, as with winemaking techniques, can change the original flavors and therefore greatly vary the choice of a suitable wine pairing. You know that winemaking techniques (apart from the other factors of climate, soil, and so on) can change the taste of the grape. Take Chardonnay, for example. If you ferment and age it in oak barrels rather than stainless steel, it will taste oakier. If full malolactic fermentation is allowed, then it will taste more buttery. This means you can't say that Chardonnay always goes with such-and-such a dish; you need to identify a particular style of

Chardonnay, such as a steely, mineral-complex Chablis, or a buttery, oaky, sweet Napa Valley.

The same is true for food. Take a hamburger. What kind of meat are you going to use for the patty? Do you buy organic, lean, fatty, or grain fed? The origin of the meat will already be a factor in the resulting texture and taste. Then, how are you going to cook it? Are you going to opt for an outdoor barbecue, sauté it in a frying pan, grill it, or roast it in the oven? Four different cooking methods produce four distinctly different tastes.

Now add the condiments. Will you use onions, garlic, Tabasco sauce, or ketchup? Will you top it with Cheddar, Swiss, or blue cheese? Perhaps you'll add some bacon and avocado. Finally, are you going to put it on a sesame seed bun or on a toasted and buttered hard roll? The final taste results are infinite. And each one of these choices could vary your final choice of wine. If your hamburger were barbecued, you might try a spicy Zinfandel, especially if the coals were mesquite. With a pan-fried hamburger, perhaps a Merlot; with blue cheese, a Cabernet-dominated Bordeaux or a heavy, oaky, slightly sweet Chardonnay.

COOKING AND PREPARATION METHODS

The way in which a food is cooked has an enormous impact on the way it will taste. Just imagine the difference between a hard-boiled egg and a fried one; a raw carrot and a boiled one; or a grilled steak and a beef stew. Two things define all cooking methods: the variations of heat, and the variations in the amount of liquid used. The more liquid used and the less heat applied, the more the food's texture is softened, and the more the flavor is intensified. The less liquid and more heat applied, the more the food's color and flavor are preserved or increased and its texture becomes crispy. To put it simply, "fast, hot, and dry" preserves taste, while "slow, moderate, and moist" intensifies flavors. And when it comes to matching wines, a general guideline is that those foods that are prepared with a light method of cooking (poaching or steaming, for example) would usually require a fruity, lightly acidic wine rather than a heavy tannic one, even if the poached food has a spicy or heavy sauce to accompany it.

Steaming
This delicate cooking method helps foods retain all their freshness, flavor, and texture by using no liquid at all, just tenderizing the food in steam. Steamed foods, such as vegetables or Oriental dishes, usually need slightly acidic, fruity white wines.

Poaching

Poaching is a very gentle simmer in liquid (try fresh oysters poached in Champagne with julienne carrots and leeks as a potage). The amount of water, stock, or wine in which the food is poached depends on the food itself. Once the food is cooked, the cooking liquid can be boiled until it has reduced, then used as the basis for a sauce. Poaching is usually used for foods with delicate textures and tastes, because this method tends to preserve both. As with steaming, it will result in a very delicate dish, regardless of flavorings, and would do well with a fruity, light- to medium-bodied wine— probably a white, as you don't see much "poached steak" on menus!

Boiling

Because boiling doesn't add flavor to foods, this method has more to do with texture than taste. It is used for tenderizing tough pieces of meat, which are submerged in water or stock at a high temperature. The flavors of the food in fact tend to be toned down, especially if the food is salty (think of that Christmas ham). The texture of boiled meat needs a medium to heavy red.

Stir-Frying

This method is most successful if performed quickly and at a very high temperature. There are many variables in this method, including the kind of fat used and the depth of the pan (from a pot to a wok). Stir-frying is primarily meant to preserve a food's color and flavor, although it does intensify the taste a little. It will produce a dish with a relatively light texture and simple flavor, compared to the heaviness and flavor complexity of a stew, for example. As the sauce is often created in the frying process, its taste will also influence the choice of wine. Usually, a light, fruity, acidic red or white is best—nothing too oaky, too tannic, or too sweet.

Deep-Frying

Despite what you might think, when you immerse foods in a large, deep pan of boiling fat, it is better to use more fat, not less. According to my *Larousse Gastronomique,* food fried in plenty of fresh hot oil is sealed immediately and therefore does not absorb the fat but becomes crisp, firm, and cooked through. When too little fat is used, on the other hand, this sealing process cannot take place, so the fat is absorbed into the food and the pieces stick to one another and become soggy. I learned this while perfecting my *frites* technique in Paris! If cooked correctly, deep-fried foods are surprisingly light and delicate and are best complemented by light, fruity, acidic wines.

Braising, Casseroling, and Stewing

Generally used for red meats, such as beef and lamb, these methods can also be applied to veal, pork, and venison. The idea is to exchange flavors, so lots of vegetables, spices, and herbs are used. Large cuts of meat can be marinated before braising because, as with boiling, this method softens the food's texture. If done slowly, the flavors of the foods are intensified. The results are complex and heavily textured, which means you can match these dishes with full, oaky whites or tannic, rustic reds.

Grilling

A method requiring very intense heat, grilling works by sealing all the nourishing juices into the meat by the crust formed on the surface. Because it is fast and does not allow time for the meat to tenderize, it is usually reserved for the best. Grilling, like roasting, uses dry heat, but it is faster than roasting. It tends to produce more intense and smoky flavors. Grilled meats need mature, full reds with tannins and heavy, dark fruit.

Roasting

Roasting is the complete opposite of steaming, poaching, and boiling because it uses dry heat to intensify the taste and add a unique flavor. The flavors are concentrated on the outside, browned layers of the meat where juices have evaporated, which gives a slightly caramelized flavor to the crusty surface—like crackling, for example. Smooth, elegant, and mature reds will best match the juicy, flavorful cuts of meat that are reserved for this most noble of methods.

THE WEIGHT OF FOOD

The cooking method employed combines with the food's weight and texture to produce the variables of taste. Faced with a tender fillet of sole, you may decide to preserve its texture and weight by steaming it, or to change its texture and weight by frying it in butter, which will make it heavier and denser. Like wine, you analyze a food's texture, weight, and consistency as well as its basic taste. You can use all of these clues to form an opinion and a match.

What I mean by "weight" is very simply the substance or heaviness of the food or dish. Compare a salad to a lamb stew that has been in your Crock-Pot overnight. The salad is the lighter dish in weight, in substance, and also in its concentration of flavors. The lamb stew is the more substantial, heavy dish. You may have put the same spices in both dishes—say basil and parsley—but that doesn't mean that the two dishes are going to take the same wine, as their respective weights will require different wines.

When matching wines to a dish's taste and weight, it is easier to match light wines to light dishes. You can also use a light wine for a heavier dish to cut through it and freshen it, although the more traditional match is a heavier, rustic wine to complement it. Imagine foie gras with a rich and sweet Sauternes, or Indian food with a spicy Gewürztraminer; these two pairings are matching food and wine of similar weights.

THE TEXTURE OF FOOD

Texture is quite a different thing to weight. Think about how a wine feels in your mouth. Is it dry and slow to go down, or heavy or smooth? Is it "puckery" because of its young tannins? Or light and crisp, due to its acidity? Perhaps it tastes round and smooth as a result of the glycerin? Imagine a light, acidic Sancerre (the Sauvignon Blanc grape) with briny, fresh oysters. Imagine a velvety Paulliac or St-Julien (Cabernet Sauvignon dominated) with a tender spring lamb roast. In these pairings, the textures of the food and wine match.

 ## MATCHING THE CATEGORIES OF TASTE, WEIGHT, AND TEXTURE

FOOD	WINE
Acidic foods	Acidic wines, fruity and aromatic, off dry
Fatty or oily foods	Acidic wines with a rich, full flavor; rosés, not tannic reds
Fishy foods	Fruity, aromatic, full-bodied, off-dry whites and rosés
Salty foods	Sweet whites; low-tannin reds
Smoked foods	Oaked, rich, and fruity whites; spicy reds
Spicy foods	Fruity, young, low-tannin, moderate-alcohol reds; whites with some residual sugar and light acidity
Sweet foods	Sweet wines of equal or more sweetness
Vinegary foods	Fruity, light, and dry or slightly sweet whites, of equal acidity

However, you can also use contrasting textures. Take our foie gras again, but this time marry it with a bubbly, crisp Pinot Noir–based Champagne. Now you have the spicy robustness of this grape contrasting with the sweet smoothness of the foie gras, and the crisp, effervescent texture of the Champagne contrasting with the rich creaminess of the foie gras. A contrasting marriage in this case is just as effective.

THE IMPORTANCE OF SAUCES

So far I have looked at the cooking method, the weight, and the texture of the food. All of these before we even get to the variable of the sauce! Imagine you have before you a poached chicken breast—a fairly innocuous beast that needs a bit of livening up. Are you going to smother it with a lemon and cream sauce? A mushroom and Marsala sauce? A tomato and onion sauce? And in that lemon and cream sauce, will you use tarragon or parsley? In the mushroom and Marsala sauce, garlic or cloves? And in the tomato and onion, basil or curry? The equation is becoming more complex, isn't it?

Sauces change not only the flavor of the dish but also its texture and weight. A sauce made with butter, olive oil, cream, or egg yolks will give the dish more body. Sauces with these bases will also be very rich and will need an acidic wine to cut through the heaviness and provide some balance. Again, there is a wide spectrum even here, with an herb butter sauce being much lighter than a béarnaise or hollandaise sauce. The former needs fruity, crisp, aromatic wines, like a minerally Chablis or a Sancerre, while the latter needs acidity, but with more substance, like an oaky Chardonnay or an Alsace Pinot Gris.

The whole thing could easily become overwhelming—but the beauty is that you are in control and can do as you like. Despite all the influences that precede it, the sauce will contain the magic clues essential for making a good wine match. Think of the sauce as the liquid seasoning for the food. Sauces usually have a base: cream, tomato, red wine, white wine, vegetable stock, or meat stock. And to these bases, you can add more layers of flavors, or you can stick to the basic ingredients.

Oil-based sauces are actually rather light and in general work well with dry red wines. An olive oil and herb sauce on pasta or roast vegetables will go nicely, not surprisingly, with a medium-weight Italian red such as Barbera. The roasted sesame oil you might use in a Chinese stir-fry works with a spicy, sweet white, not only because the oil is light, but also because the spices used in the stir-fry are best with a richer, honeyed, fruity wine. Spicy, sweetish whites, such as a Gewürztraminer, will also complement the soy sauce used in Chinese cooking; a wine that has a lot of tannin or is very oaky would become even drier and coarser on the palate with a salty sauce such as soy. Fruity whites and rosés with a touch of sweetness will temper the saltiness and keep the textures balanced. Hazelnut and walnut oils used in salads need oaky, fruity whites like a New World Chardonnay.

Barbecued sauces need a sweet, warm-climate red such as a Zinfandel or Shiraz, because the warm fruit is sweetish and the tannins can hold up to such a sauce, where a sweetish white would be crushed. Oak-dominated reds would not do so well, however, so stick to the fruit.

Tomato sauces and vegetable purees used as a sauce are usually on the acidic side and so need an acidic yet fruitier counterbalance, such as a Sauvignon Blanc, or a fruity red Italian, or a Merlot if there is meat in the sauce.

You will find specific sauce and wine matches in the Sauces listing in part 3.

After establishing the base of the sauce, the next step is usually adding the herb or spice dimensions. Although these are carefully chosen to match the sauce's base, they often end up with a starring role. Try putting curry with coconut milk. The milk will sweeten it a bit, but there will be no mistaking that the curry is the dominant flavor of the sauce, and of the dish.

SPICES, HERBS, AND CONDIMENTS

Who can deny the historical, cultural, and economic impact that the spice trade has had on the world? Spices have always been more than a simple seasoning. They were associated with wealth, exotic travel, the discovery of new continents, sovereignty, and power. From the East came sailing ships laden with spices, textiles, and perfumes to the great empires of Greece, Rome, Mesopotamia, Arabia, and Egypt.

Long before the Christian era, Greek merchants thronged the markets of southern India. Epicurean Rome spent a fortune on Indian spices, silks, and brocades. It is said that Rome fought the Parthian Wars largely to keep open the trade route to India, and that there may have been no Crusades and no expeditions to the East without the lure of Indian spices. Spices were such royal luxuries that men were willing to risk their lives for them. This is hard to believe when spices cost so little today.

And what did they use the spices for? To enhance and vary the taste of their foods, certainly, and also to mask the taste of food that was slightly off and would otherwise be thrown away. Some spices were also used for pre-serving meat and other food without refrigeration. Cloves, for example, were a popular preservative in the sixteenth century. They contain a chemical called eugenol, which inhibits the growth of bacteria, and are still used to preserve some modern foods like Virginia ham. (When you run out of mints, try sucking on a clove for a few minutes to freshen your breath quickly and make your mouth feel great.) If spices were not available, then food could not be preserved during the winter months and there would be nothing to eat—that is how important they were historically.

Spices also can be used as antioxidants, as they possess antibiotic prop-erties. They intensify saliva flow and the secretion of amylase, neuraminic acid, and hexosamines. They clean food and bacteria from the mouth and may even help prevent infection and cavities. They also protect the mucus in the mouth against thermic, mechanical, and chemical irritation. Spices increase the secretion of saliva rich in ptyalin, which facilitates starch diges-tion in the stomach, making carbohydrate-rich meals more digestible. Spices may also activate the adrenocortical function and fortify resistance and phys-ical capacity. The risk of stroke and high blood pressure can be markedly diminished or augmented by means of spices. Indeed, the medicinal uses of herbs and spices would fill another book, but are not the topic under dis-cussion here.

What Are Spices?

Spices shape a people's culinary personality. Both are products of a par-ticular place and its environment. The climate dictates which spices and plants will thrive in the area. A hot climate will produce some pretty fiery-tasting spices and thus infuse both cuisine and entire culture with a similar personality! Subconsciously, we associate countries with their family of spices—it suits them. Mention chile peppers and you can immediately imagine yourself lying on a beach in Mexico with a glass of chilled tequi-la. And before you can finish saying allspice or cinnamon, I am on that French ski slope sipping my mulled wine and brushing up my après-ski skills. (Let's forget the fact that these spices, like most others, are indigenous to tropical climates. We are permitted such daydreams because they have been in Europe since the ninth and tenth centuries—long enough to allow a bit of poetic license.)

Technically, a spice, or condiment, is an aromatic plant with no per-manent woody stem above the ground. Spices and condiments are natural plants, vegetable products, or mixtures of the two, in whole or ground form, which are used for imparting flavor, aroma, and piquancy to foods. Since spices may be comprised of different plant components or parts, you can assume that herbs are then part of spices and condiments, and I will group them all together here for the sake of clarity . . . and brevity!

There are about seventy known spices grown in different parts of the world. This variety lies in the fact that a spice can vary not only by the plant from which it originates, but also by the different parts of the plant—each one having its unique taste. So, where with wine we were concerned with the aromas located in and under the skin, here we faced with even more infinitesimal choices!

Why such a lengthy discussion of spices? Because they form the basis of our argument. They are the primary ingredients used to flavor food and are often the dominant base of a dish to which you are trying to match a wine. They are indispensable to the culinary art. Spices are to food what grape varieties are to wine. Basic ingredient meets basic ingredient.

 ## THE BOTANY OF SPICES AND HERBS

Here are the principal parts of a plant and some well-known examples of spices and herbs produced from them.

PART OF PLANT	SPICES AND HERBS
Aril	Mace
Bark	Cinnamon and cassia
Berries	Allspice, black pepper, and juniper
Bulbs	Garlic and onion
Flowers	Cloves and saffron
Fruit	Cardamom and chiles
Leaves	Bay leaves, mint, and marjoram
Kernel	Nutmeg
Rhizomes	Ginger and turmeric
Roots	Angelica, horseradish, and lovage
Seeds	Aniseed, caraway, celery, and coriander

 CLASSIFYING SPICES AND HERBS

According to *Larousse Gastronomique,* all condiments (which are of vegetable origin) are classified by their dominant flavor. This is the classification the cooking authority applies:

FLAVOR	SPICES AND HERBS
Salty	Sea salt
Acidic	Vinegar, verjuice, lemon juice, capers, sea fennel, nasturtiums
Bitter	Garlic, shallots, onions, mustard, horseradish
Bitter aromatic	Paprika, dill, anise, basil, coffee, cinnamon, chervil, coriander, cumin, turmeric, tarragon, fennel, juniper, clove, bay, mace, mint, nutmeg, parsley, saffron, sage, thyme, vanilla
Sweet	Sugar, honey
Fat	Oils, butters, fats

THE COMPONENTS OF SPICES AND HERBS

Even in something as apparently invariable as a spice or herb, there are qualitative requirements, and climate, soil, and yields are of great importance. Herbs and spices, like vine plants, do not do well with too many fertilizers or manures. Like the vine, they just need the appropriate soil, moisture, and light, and each one has a natural habitat or climatic origin. If you really want to get carried away, you could use fresh spices imported from their native lands, but most of us are happy enough to grow them on our windowsills or to stick with the cultivated variety found in jars in the local supermarket.

We know that spices and herbs, while very healthful, are not considered to have any nutritional value. For example, a dry bay leaf has the following composition: moisture, protein, fat, fiber, carbohydrates, total ash, calcium, phosphorus, sodium, potassium, iron. It also contains the following vitamins per 100 milligrams: 0.10 mg of vitamin B_1 (thiamin); 0.42 mg of vitamin B_2 (riboflavin); 2.0 mg of vitamin B_6 (niacin); 46.6 mg of vitamin C (ascorbic acid); 545 international units of vitamin A. And it contains 410 calories per 100 grams.

HERBS, SPICES, AND WINES

When my husband, a London restaurateur, was helping edit this book, he couldn't help but smile at some of the food and wine matches. "Who sits down to a plate of coriander? Or a bowl of asparagus? According to this, we would need a different wine for each foodstuff and each spice on the plate—which brings Sunday lunch up to a grand total of about fifteen different wines!—a sip with the potatoes, another sip with the roast and gravy, yet another with the horseradish sauce!"

In case you may have been thinking along the same lines, I'll clarify. The point is that although you may not be eating a dish of bay leaves, you understand that when they are the dominant flavor of the dish, they have a specific effect. And as for the asparagus, my husband's chef just put the most delicious Parmesan and asparagus tarts on the menu—a perfect lunch with a side salad—so now we do indeed have to know which wine goes with asparagus and Parmesan.

Herbs add to the savory dimension of a dish and make the dish a little more interesting for the wine. Many wines even have spicy or herbal notes to them and thus are natural accompaniments. Obviously, the amount of the herb used will determine the extent of its flavoring. The way in which it is used is also important. If the herbs are used in a bouquet garni and infused in a big pot of stock, then the flavors will gently permeate whatever you are cooking. But if you take the same herbs and grill or roast them along with your meat, then their influence becomes much heavier and you will need a more assertive and up-front wine, less complex and subtle than that you would use for the former dish.

Herbs and spices can also alter the taste and texture of wine, and that's where the matching comes in. Some clash with tannins or oaks, while others—such as chile, mustard, or horseradish—simply blitz the palate and numb the taste buds, let alone what they might do to the wine. Another factor to consider is that a lot of the spices and herbs used in international cuisine are from countries where wine is not produced, so it is no wonder that finding a suitable match might be difficult. Although this book is about food and wine, do not be shy if you prefer beer with your Thai, tequila with your Mexican, or vodka with your Russian.

When matching herbs to wine, we are trying to complement the herbal notes often found in wine. When matching spices with wine, we are trying to temper the dish from crushing the palate and the wine. Herbs are a much easier affair. They add more flavor, complexity, and dimension to a dish, rather than dominating it as a spice will do. Herbs can be sweet, bitter, pungent, and either subtle or assertive, depending on your cooking method. They do best with warm, acidic reds or herbal acidic whites. Spices always seem to clash with a wine, and sweet and spicy whites are your best answer in most cases. I think the best strategy, and the one I subconsciously employed while composing the chart below, is to take into account the region or origin of the herb or spice, to imagine which dishes it is most traditionally used in, and then work from there. I didn't "just know" that basil would go with a Chianti or Barolo, I simply imagined a plate of steaming fettuccine in pesto sauce and went from there to search for a fruity, lively, and vibrant red as a match—and I didn't have to go very far!

 MATCHING HERBS, SPICES, AND WINES

SPICE OR HERB	WINE TYPE	WINE EXAMPLE
Basil	Fruity, acidic red, or crisp, dry white (no oak)	Chianti, Nebbiolo, Orvieto, Soave
Bay	Young red	Barbera, Chianti
Capers	Dry, acidic, slightly sweet white	Riesling, Sauvignon Blanc
Chiles	Fruity, low-tannin, and low-oak red	Beaujolais, Dolcetto, Merlot
Cinnamon	Spicy, warm, mature red	Merlot, Pomerol, Pinot Noir, Shiraz
Coriander	Fresh, green, crisp white, or warm, rustic red	Sauvignon Blanc, Riesling, Syrah
Cumin seed	Fruity, aromatic white	Sauvignon Blanc, Riesling
Dill	Fresh, green, crisp white	Sauvignon Blanc, Soave
Fennel	Full-bodied, warm white, or light, acidic red	Viognier, Barbera, St-Véran
Garlic	Dry, herby white or rosé	Côtes du Rhône, Bandol rosé
Ginger	Sweet, young white with good acids	Barsac, Gewürztraminer, Muscat
Horseradish	Fruity, lightly acidic white, or light red	Sancerre, Dolcetto, Beaujolais
Juniper	Spicy, full red	Zinfandel, Mourvèdre
Mint	Minty, herby, richly fruity red	Cabernet Sauvignon
Mustard	Solid, acidic white	Sancerre, Moselle, Riesling

SPICE OR HERB	WINE TYPE	WINE EXAMPLE
Nutmeg	Spicy, mature red	Burgundy, New World Pinot Noir
Oregano	Spicy, earthy red, or acidic white	Sauvignon Blanc
Parsley	Spicy, earthy red, or acidic white	Sauvignon Blanc
Pepper	Tannic, rustic red	Cabernet Sauvignon, Côtes du Rhône
Rosemary	Robust, rustic red	Syrah, Bandol, Fitou, Barolo
Saffron	Full or sweet white, or fruity red	Merlot, Barsac, Vouvray, Chardonnay
Sage	Fruity, oaky, slightly sweetish, light red	New World Merlot, Alentejo
Tarragon	Smooth, slightly sweet, oaky white	Chardonnay, Chenin Blanc
Thyme	Spicy, earthy red or acidic white	Sauvignon Blanc
Vanilla	Sweet, spicy white	Pacherenc du Vic-Bilh, Tokàji

THE DIVERSITY OF INTERNATIONAL CUISINES

We know to look to regional wines to match our food in countries like France, Italy, and Germany. The exercise is also viable when extended to the New World but the rules change a bit, for not only is the wine new in these countries, but so is the culinary scene, insofar as they are cultural melting pots. Immigration, emigration, foreign travel, and other factors have all made for original and fresh cuisines, and they have produced a whole new genre of cuisine with myriad exotic spices, textures, and flavors called Mediterrasian, Modern British, fusion, or Pacific Rim. Still, we have no problem figuring out that red Burgundy would suit a coq au vin; a California red Zinfandel would beautifully complement a venison steak with juniper and sweet potatoes; and a Chilean Merlot makes a great companion for empanadas.

But what about those countries that either do not produce their own wines or produce too little to be relevant outside the specific regions? (You won't find a bottle of Chinese Rkatsiteli on the shelf at your local A&P!) Sadly, their cuisine is sometimes relegated to the category of take-out food, but these cuisines are as multidimensional, complex, and diverse as those with which we are most familiar. China, for example, is a vast country with indigenous cooking styles in its many different regions. It, too, has its Alsace, Burgundy, and Bordeaux, even though the average consumer only knows of the stereotyped, generic favorites. Authentic Chinese dishes are a riot of texture, color, and contrasting flavors, and we can often find a whole range of taste sensations in a single dish. What follows is a brief overview of the dominant flavors in the dishes of these countries. For specific dishes and their wine matches, see part 3.

In general, Oriental dishes are hot (using chiles and peppers), salty (from the soy and oyster sauces), sweet (with sugar and honey), and sour (from the use of vinegar). Pick out the dominant flavor in the dish and match that to the dominant characteristics in the wine. You will find, however, that often even spicy or bitter dishes have a sweetish backbone and need wines with low tannins; this is why whites work so well. Also try dry rosés and sparkling wines.

Serving Wine During a Meal

Here are some guidelines on how to serve wines from different regions at the same meal.

- Chilled wines come before room-temperature wines.
- Younger wines are served before older ones.
- Lighter wines come before heavier, coarser ones.
- White wines before reds.
- Red wines before sweet white wines (unless the sweet white wine has been served as an aperitif or with a first course like foie gras).

Wines served from the same wine region should be served in order of vintage, the younger before the old, even if the younger is a better growth—although there may, of course, be a few exceptions to this.

The idea is to save the heaviest, more complex wines for last so as not to spoil the palate for lighter wine.

Chinese Food

Chinese food is a lot more than chicken chow mein and crispy noodles. The dominant flavors are ginger, garlic, spring onions, soy sauce, salt, sugar, pepper, chiles, roasted sesame oil, oyster sauce, and coriander. The resulting sauces are sweet-and-sour, peanut, ginger, and oyster—all of which fall into either the sweet or the salty taste group.

This means that your best matches are going to be sweetish, spicy, or fruity white wines with a bit of residual sugar. If reds are matched, choose low-tannin, unoaked reds (especially with duck dishes), because salty foods make a wine's tannins taste more bitter. Acidic wines are also a bad idea unless you have a fatty duck dish that can take it. And oaked wines are not a good idea unless the dish contains smoked meats. A slightly oaked Chardonnay would, however, work with sesame-based sauces or a peanut sauce. Or try an Alsatian Gewürztraminer with the ginger and peanut sauces, and a slightly sweet Vouvray, New World Chardonnay, or Sémillon with most others. Light, crisp rosés and sparkling wines also are a very good match, as their texture can either cut through any heaviness in a dish or underline the delicacy of the more fragile ones, such as wontons and other steamed dumplings.

China has about ninety wineries and the recent focus, after decades of sweet white wines made from unpronounceable hybrids, is medium-dry whites for domestic and foreign consumption.

Japanese Food

The overall flavors of Japanese cuisine are bitter and vinegary: Think of wasabi (green horseradish), vinegar, soy sauces, and onions.

When serving wine with Japanese food, avoid acidic wines and go for chilled, off-dry, fruity white wines and any sparkling wines with most dishes like sashimi or sushi. For the slightly heavier dishes, such as tempura or *yakitorri* (grilled chicken and chicken livers with spring onions), choose fuller, fruitier styles: red Chinon, Saumur, or Sancerre would work. Again, good brut Champagne will always save the day.

White wine grapes (Koshu) have been grown near Mount Fuji since 1186! But the rest of Japan's annual 7,220,000 cases are an odd mix of European-style wines from European varieties that sadly tend to be characterless and diluted due to the heavy rainfall in the region. Worth trying, however, is Suntory's Château Lion, a sweet white of botrytized Sémillon; but it is very expensive.

Thai Food

Thai food uses aromatic, spicy flavors, and its playful contrasting tastes make it very difficult to match indeed. Thai food indulges in generous heaps of fresh chiles, lime leaves, lemongrass, citrus juices, coriander, ginger, and basil, just to name a few. The antidote here is crisp, dry whites, not spicy, slightly sweet ones. Try New World Sauvignon Blanc, Marsanne, or Chardonnay for creamy curries, biranis, and even meat satays. A fruity, robust Shiraz will do very nicely with chile and beef dishes. My favorite—as you may have already guessed—is a brut Champagne.

Mexican Food

Another very difficult cuisine to match with wine, Mexican food is chile dominated—the Aztecs' love of beans, chile, and corn inspired modern Mexican cooking—and everyone will tell you that chile does not affect the wine, only your palate, burning it until you cannot tell water from molasses.

Very hot and spicy foods need equally spicy wines with a touch of residual sugar to counteract the spice. Try chilled, fruity whites and acidic rosés to temper all that heat. Low-tannin reds that are fruity and spicy like New World Merlot or Pinot Noir, or a good Beaujolais Cru, will also work. Apart from the chiles, the Mexican diet seems to contain a lot of corn flour and beef—tamales, chili con carne, chili con queso, carnitas. Mexicans usually accompany their meals with beer, tequila, or chocolate drinks.

The irony of Mexico is that it has been producing wine since the end of the nineteenth century but because it was considered too hot for wine, 80 percent of the harvest goes directly into brandy and vermouth production. You might be surprised to know that international companies such as Domecq, Freixenet, Hennessy, Martell, Suntory, Seagram, and Cinzano have all heavily invested in Mexico for their brandy trade. Despite this, the wines have become more serious since 1980 and are increasingly being relocated to cooler plateaus or coastal regions.

Indian Food

Think Indian and you think curry, curry, and more curry. The basic staple of Indian cuisine is the rice and wheat for the doshai, chapatis, and paratha breads. There is also a great variety of vegetables and fruit; the coconut is used both for its milk and its flesh. And while, yes, curry seems to be a common denominator, let's not forget chile, turmeric, coriander, mustard seeds, ginger, cloves, cinnamon, pepper, cumin, lime, tamarind, yogurt, cardamom, and fennel.

All these spices, which are usually incorporated in a creamy yogurt- or milk-based sauce, need wines of low alcohol and tannin content that are fruity and sweet—and with definitely no oak. Straightforward Merlots, Zinfandels, and Syrahs can work. Try a full-bodied rosé from Bordeaux with samosas and pakoras, or Gewürztraminer with tandoori. Try full-bodied sparkling wines—rosé Champagne for example. If you can find it, try Indian sparkling wine.

Until the Portuguese came along in the fifteenth century, the Indians had two thousand years of haphazard winemaking under their belt. Now the 167,000 cases produced annually are rather decent modern imitations of the European models.

Middle Eastern Food

The exotic perfumes of figs, raisins, cinnamon, nuts, and turmeric are warm and sweet. Soft, fruity reds and whites complement Middle Eastern flavors best, and although our rule of matching sweet food with sweet wine still applies, it needs to be done carefully. The texture and weight of Middle Eastern food can render some sweet wines too heavy; the entire meal loses its nuances and becomes sickeningly sweet. Try Beaujolais and New World Pinot Noir and Château Musar, Lebanon's masterpiece of Cabernet Sauvignon/Cinsault.

Mediterrasian, Pacific Rim, Modern British Food

This most trendy of cusines is rather easier to match with wine than you might think. Certainly there are no safe local or regional wines to refer to, and every single spice and condiment imaginable can be used in a same dish, sometimes in a very confrontational manner. The goal is to surprise, wake up, and startle.

Not much room for a wine in all of that, you might say. But the best complements to all of these outspoken dishes are the equally outspoken and up-front New World varietals. The new style is to take the Old World classic staples and "sunkiss" them to the extreme: We want everything to taste, look, and smell as though it has just been picked under a high-noon sun. My husband calls it "zapping the taste buds."

I like to think that the popularity of this new cuisine, along with the revival of ethnic cuisine, is in response to our modern culture and the fact that our attention spans have seriously lessened. We are, and you've surely heard this before, the generation of instant gratification. After four bites (one = inquiry, two = confirmation, three = satisfaction, four = indulgence), we want to move on to something else. Ethnic foods, with their varied spices and numerous small dishes, fit the bill perfectly. Ask friends to dig their way through a bowl of game casserole and they lose interest halfway through. The idea is to take the basics of a traditional cuisine and simplify yet magnify the dominant flavors—for example, the American/Italian marriage called "Cal-Ital." We seem to have embraced the entire Mediterranean basin, so the obvious vinous mate will be the big, obvious, exaggerated, hot-climate varietals: a Syrah, a Merlot, a Cabernet Sauvignon, a Chardonnay, or a Sauvignon Blanc.

As the U.K. editor of the Paris wine magazine *Vintage,* I was able to participate in food and wine "experiments" as research for our cuisine articles, usually by Elizabeth de Meurville, the French food writer. She would call a chef and explain what she wanted to experiment with: oysters and wines at Cap Vernet, Côtes du Rhônes chez Guy Savoy, or Loires chez Jean Bardet in Tours. It was strenuous, believe it or not, keeping up with her and the magical combinations placed before us, but we were up to the challenge. She has taught me a great deal about food. There were also the weekly, if not daily, lunches and dinners hosted by château owners: another comprehensive exercise in food and wine pairings.

With hundreds of wines a week as homework, my palate was and still is, continually being worked out. I couldn't begin to list my favorite discoveries—they would fill a book themselves!—but here a few worth mentioning:

- *Coquilles St-Jacques des Côtes d'Armor aux senteurs pérogourdines* (layers of scallops, foie gras, and truffles in filo pastry) with Chablis Premier Cru Côte de l'Chetî 1990. Tirel-Guérin Restaurant, St-Meloir des Ondes (near St-Malo), February 1994.
- *Risotto aux morilles* (morel risotto) with Bandol Rouge Château Pibarnon 1985. Prepared by and enjoyed with Alain Ducasse Louis IV, Monte Carlo, the day he became the only chef in the world to have two Michelin three-star restaurants, spring 1997.
- *Saumon mi-fumé, poêlé sur barbe de capucin, vinaigrette au jus de betteraves* (partially smoked salmon pan-fried on a bed of nasturtiums with a beetroot juice vinaigrette) with Château de France Bordeaux Blanc 1993. Hôtel Ritz, April 1996.

> - *Gâteau de pommes de terre au foie gras* (potato pancakes with foie gras) with Château Lascombes 1985 and 1992. Carré des Feuillants, chez Alain Dutournier, April 1996.
> - *Blanquette de sole coquilles St-Jacques au jus de cerfeuil, concombre et gingembre* (blanquette of sole and scallops with a chervil, cucumber, and ginger sauce) with Champagne Gosset Celebris. Hôtel de Brissac, September 1995.

MATCHING FOOD AND WINE

If I may, I wish to quote Matt Kramer *(Making Sense of Wine)* quoting prolific wine and food writer Richard Olney (1986 interview in the *Wine Spectator*): "The general mode of thinking always leans on the cliché and on the abstract. People do not return to their palates. People are afraid that they do not know how to taste. They prefer to lean on rules. With rules you don't have to think; you don't have to taste. You just have to follow the rules—and they'll destroy you every time."

Was he talking only of food and wine?!

What an appropriate way in which to begin the section on food and wine pairing guidelines! Can we really say that there are no rules? I don't think so. Perhaps what might best be said is that taste is subjective, so that a combination a certain individual might put together because he or she likes it is then, by definition, an acceptable pairing. Because putting personal, subjective taste aside, there are rules. Nobody sat down and wrote them up; they are simply laws of nature, of chemistry. Acid and bitter tastes reinforce each other. Sweet tastes change acidic and bitter tastes, as well as salty tastes. (Sweet wines with salty foods work—whereas tannic or alcohol reds with salty foods taste bitter.) The bitterness and acidity of a tannic red wine will make fish or creamy cheese taste metallic. Now, if you happen to enjoy the taste of a copper penny on your tongue—go for it. Because Mr. Olney is quite right in that you should taste something for yourself rather than let someone decide for you.

If in a match, both personalities are distinct yet compatible, success has been achieved, and if in a match, both personalities are not only distinct and compatible but also draw out the hidden tastes or qualities of the other, then nirvana has been reached. In fact, matching food and wine is very much analogous to finding your soul mate. Not an easy task, but certainly an enjoyable exercise.

Food as an Enemy

When we say that a particular food item or dish is an enemy to wine, we mean that it alters detrimentally the taste of wine. From one of my oldest copies of the *Larousse Gastronomique* in its original French: *"Nous n'indiquons de vins ni pour les potages ni pour les oeufs; seuls conviennent de petits vins de carafe. Avec les crudités et les salades, il est préférable de boire un verre d'eau fraîche."* In other words, soups and eggs only merit carafe wines, and a glass of fresh water is the only solution for raw vegetables and salads. Not true, not true! Where is their imagination? There is always a solution to these culinary quandaries, and at the risk of repeating myself, there is always Champagne!

What follows are some guidelines to some classic friends and foes of wine. For specific recipe and wine matches, refer to part 3.

Grilled and Poached Seafood or Shellfish

Dry whites are the perfect match in texture, weight, and flavor to poached seafood or shellfish, while dry rosés are perfect for the grilled dishes. Try whites such as Entre-Deux-Mers, Graves, Chablis, Pouilly-Fuissé for poached fish, and slightly more flavorful whites such as a Condrieu (Viognier), New Zealand Sauvignon Blanc, or California Chardonnay for those that are grilled. Tasty rosés such as Tavel, Cassis, Bandol, and Lirac are also good, slightly heavier or more full-bodied matches.

Fish in Sauce

For fish in sauces, the matches above still apply. But if the sauce has a bit of personality and spice in it, you will need whites that also have a bit more character, such as Meursault, white Hermitage, Riesling, and, again, most of the New World Chardonnays and Sauvignon Blancs. If the sauce is a bit sweet, a Vouvray, Coteaux du Layon, or Monbazillac can be spectacular. Fish in a red wine sauce works if the fish is meaty, like monkfish, tuna, or swordfish, and if the red wine is light or medium bodied, like a Merlot or an Italian Barbera.

Oysters

If ever there was an unlikely, fraught relationship, this is it. With their high levels of salt and acid, and pronounced flavor of the sea, oysters have a reputation for killing wines. Oysters, like wines, have "producers" and "growths." Furthermore, their taste can vary enormously depending on their size (and therefore age) and, especially, on the *terroir* and the method used to raise them. Oysters can vary greatly in texture and taste: They can be salty and wiry, sweet and fleshy, or meatlike and complex. Good oysters, like good wine, are not even commercialized until they are three years old. And unlike other food and wine matches, it is the oyster that might dominate a wine.

The predictable conclusion in this match is to serve oysters not with a very expensive *grand vin* but rather with a well-made and sufficiently powerful wine, such as a Sancerre. Expensive wines are too refined and subtle to emerge unscathed from such an encounter with the flavor of the ocean. The Sauvignon Blanc stands up to the opponent beautifully. Other perfect matches are Muscadet or Riesling (a crisp, fresh one), or a white Bordeaux, such as a Graves. What shouldn't you drink? White Côtes du Rhône, Sylvaner, and Chardonnays seem to go flat and bitter.

Grilled White Meats

Grilled white meats like chicken breast, turkey, or pork need smooth reds that are not coarse or rustic. Try a Saumur-Champigny or Chinon (Loire), a Volnay or Beaune (Burgundy), a Médoc or Chinon. This is because although a white meat may take a white wine, the cooking method means that the dish can move up to a red, but only if it is soft, smoothly textured, and of low tannin content. Rustic, big, tannic reds would dominate the white meat, even if grilled.

White Meats in White Wine Sauce

Ideally, make your sauce using the same wine you serve with the meal. White wines that lend themselves to creamy mushroom sauces for meat are Champagne, Meursault, Graves, Sauternes, and Riesling. A trick might be to use a reasonably priced, good-quality Chardonnay for the cooking, but a better Burgundy, like the Meursault, for the drinking. Most of us cannot really afford to throw a bottle of Meursault into the saucepan!

White Meats in Red Wine Sauce

Fruity, moderately tannic, and moderately alcoholic reds work best with white meats: Chambertin, Beaujolais, Chinon, Bourgueil, and St-Emilion all work well. As you can see, the common denominator is not the grape variety, as the above wines represent Pinot Noir, Gamay, Cabernet Sauvignon, Cabernet Franc, and others. It has more to do with the fruitiness and slightly acidic background that keeps the texture and flavors light enough for the meat.

Grilled or Roasted Red Meats

Grilled or roasted red meats are not difficult to match. Think Sunday roast and July barbecues; think full, ripe, and mature; think Pomerol, New World Cabernet Sauvignons and Syrahs, Cornas, Hermitage, Châteauneuf-du-Pape, St-Emilion, and Zinfandel. Both the red meat and the methods of grilling and roasting can take heavier textures and weights, so bring on the tannins, acids, and ripe fruit. No fresh, young things allowed here!

Stews and Casseroles

Stews and casseroles can handle the same sort of reds as grilled red meat, only there is a slight nuance to respect. Long, slow cooking really seals in the flavor of the meat and whatever flavorings are used, changing the meat's texture. Stews have more complex flavoring and texture, and therefore your red wine should be a bit more coarse or rustic. Try a Bordeaux Supérieur, Fronsac, or Cahors instead of a St-Emilion or Pomerol; a Santenay or Mercurey instead of a Beaune; a Côtes du Rhône instead of a Hermitage or Châteauneuf-du-Pape. New World reds might be too fruity and one dimensional for a stew, which would render them thin and weak. Stick to inexpensive classics from southwest France.

Salad with Vinegar-Based Dressing

The solution here is to use lemon juice instead of vinegar in the dressing and add protein ingredients such as cheese and nuts to balance the wine. But if you have made the salad and are staring at a plate of vinegar, remember to match a fruity, aromatic, but lightly dry white wine with equal acidity as the dressing. Sauvignon Blanc, either as a New World varietal or in the guise of a Loire Valley wine, will do nicely.

When making your own salad, choose the young leaves of the salad, as older leaves will dominate the wine. The salad leaves you choose will also have an effect. Bitter salad leaves, such as rocket, need more acidic wines than, say, iceberg lettuce. Again, the ingredients as well as the dressing will have a lot to do with the wine you choose, as you will see in part 3.

Eggs

While you may not wish to drink a glass of wine at 9 A.M. with your boiled egg and toast, by noon your eggs Benedict, quiche, soufflé, and egg-based béarnaise or hollandaise are all crying out for some vinous sustenance. Eggs are not such an enemy as you might think. Sparkling wine is perfect for the soft texture of most egg dishes, and it won't overpower their subtle, delicate flavors.

Smoked Foods

When foods are correctly smoked, their personalities are not extinguished (excuse the pun!); the smoke simply adds another texture and flavor dimension. Even the type of wood should be considered. Oak seems to be preferred because it best lends itself to the subtleties of most foods and wines. The two methods, cold- and hot-smoking, give entirely different tastes. Cold-smoking, or curing, is when the smoke simply coats the food, which is not allowed to cook. Hot-smoking, on the other hand, cooks the food and gives it a smoky flavor by raising the temperature. The thinly sliced smoked salmon that we are all most familiar with should be cold-smoked and does very well with an unoaked Chardonnay, such as steely Chablis. Actually, most smoked food is ideal with very lightly oaked or unoaked wines. Smoked shellfish is still rather unusual. You really have to acquire a taste for it—and wouldn't we rather eat fresh, anyway? That said, if you find that a smoked oyster has found its way onto your plate, wash it down with a grassy New World Sauvignon Blanc.

Meat and poultry are often marinated before being smoked, so it is a good idea to find out what was used for the marinade. If that is not possible, try a Pinotage, Zinfandel, or Shiraz, as the more subtle flavors of a more complex blend would be completely dominated. Smoked cream cheese is one of my favorites, and although I might put a rich white wine with a cream cheese, I wouldn't when it is smoked. The rich blackcurrant and gentle tannins of mature and classic Bordeaux would be perfect.

Mushrooms

A classic in my book. What I'm assuming here is that the mushrooms are on their own as a separate side dish; if they are in a wine sauce, the wine in the sauce would give us our lead. If we knew our mushrooms a bit better, we would have an easier time marrying them to dishes and wines for our sauces. There are so many different sorts of mushroom, and you just know that I am going to mention the words *terroir* and *climate* again. I am, and I am going to add another: *season*. Are you eating morels in the spring, girolles (a highly prized form of the chanterelle mushroom) and meadow agaric in the summer, or cèpes, field mushrooms (agaric), craterelles, pieds-de-mouton, lactarius, royal agaric (Caesar's mushroom), and other wild treasures in the autumn? Not to mention the various cousins that are at their peak year-round!

With mushrooms, cooking method becomes important, as it can greatly alter their taste and texture. There are as many different ways of preparing them as there are varieties: fricasseed with garlic or shallots, gilded in butter, draped in cream, in soup, in pastry, in quiches, as a garnish for meat or

MUSHROOMS AND WINE

MUSHROOM	WINE	WINE REGION	WINE STYLE
Cèpes	Pauillac	Bordeaux	Dry red
	St-Emilion	Bordeaux	Dry red
Chanterelles	Bergerac	Southwest France	Dry red
	Saumur-Champigny	Loire	Dry red
Girolles	Bergerac	Southwest France	Dry red
	Fronsac	Bordeaux	Dry red
	Mercurey	Burgundy	Dry red
Greek mushroom dishes			
	Anjou	Loire	Dry red
	Côtes de Provence rosé	Provence	Dry rosé
Morels	Cahors	Southwest France	Dry red
	Champagne	Champagne	Sparkling
	Meursault	Burgundy	Dry white
Mushrooms (general)			
	Echezeaux	Burgundy	Dry red
	Pinot Noir	New World	Dry red
	Pinotage	South Africa	Dry red
	Volnay	Burgundy	Dry red
Pleurottes	Arbois rosé	Jura	Dry rosé
	Mercurey	Burgundy	Dry red
Porcini (see also Cèpes and Wild mushrooms)			
	Gattinara	Italy	Dry red
Wild mushrooms	Syrah	Rhône or New World	Dry red
	Valdepeñas	Spain	Dry red
	Vosne-Romanée	Burgundy	Dry red

fish, as part of the sauce for chicken, liver, or kidneys, or in an omelette or scrambled eggs. Then there are the varied textures of plumpness and tenderness, the intensity of one variety or the delicacy of another, the sharpness of some types, the earthiness of very lightly cooked young mushrooms, the fleshy aromas of riper mushrooms. The flavors are infinite and the choice of wine depends very much on the particular dish. Another factor to be considered is the style of the meal. Is it a rustic family dinner or a sophisticated soirée?

Use the cooking method (mushrooms fried up in a quick cream sauce versus mushrooms cooked overnight in a stew) as your first guide, spices as your second. Generally, mushrooms require an elegant wine, despite the dish or preparation method. A robust red wine whose tannins are silky is the best idea. There are a few whites that might work: ones of character, strength, and a certain distinctiveness such as a Jura, an Arbois Vin Jaune, a white Côtes du Rhône, or a mature, full-bodied Meursault or other white Burgundy.

Cheese

There are so many different-flavored and -textured cheeses that it is impossible to make a blanket wine suggestion. Fruity red wines kill the flavorful hard cheeses, while tannic red wines kill the creamier cheeses. Your best bet is usually whites, both dry and sweet. Try dry whites with goat's cheese and sweet whites with blue cheese. If I had to offer any rule of thumb, I would suggest matching cheese to its local wines, as cheese is very faithful to its home *terroir* and climate.

 CHEESE AND WINE

CHEESE	REGION OF ORIGIN	WINE STYLE
Appenzell	Switzerland	Full-bodied Syrah or Shiraz
Asiago d'Allevo	Italy	Oaky New World Chardonnay
Baby Bel	France	Light Beaujolais-style red
Bavarian Blue (Cambozola)	Bavaria, Germany	Dry Riesling
Beaufort	Haute Savoie, France	Lightly oaked Chardonnay, Meursault, Chasselas
Beenleigh Blue	Devon, England	Port
Bel Paese	Italy	Light Chardonnay or Barbera

CHEESE	REGION OF ORIGIN	WINE STYLE
Bleu d'Auverne	Auvergne, France	Sauternes, Touraine Sauvignon
Bleu de Bresse	Burgundy, France	Light to medium reds, Fleurie, Mâcon
Bleu de Gex Haut Jura	Jura, France	White Burgundy, Arbois, Ponsard
Bonchester	Scotland	Merlot, Bordeaux
Boursault	Normandy, France	Rioja
Boursin	France	Sancerre, Sauvignon Blanc
Brebis	France	Cahors, Buzet, Pacherenc du Vic-Bilh
Brie	France	Full Chardonnay, German dessert wines, Pomerol
Brillat Savarin	Normandy, France	Champagne
Bridamour	Corsica, France	Provence red
Cabrales	Spain	Oloroso Sherry, red or white Rioja
Caerphilly	Wales	Sweet white Rioja
Camembert	Normandy, France	Normandy cider, Médoc, Côtes du Rhône, Corbières, Bandol
Cantal	Auvergne, France	Rioja, Côtes de Provence rosé, St-Pourçain
Cashel Blue	Ireland	Light fruity red
Cave Cheese	Denmark	White mature Burgundy
Chabichou du Poitou	Loire, France	New World Sauvignon Blanc, spicy Cabernet Franc
Chaource	Champagne, France	Champagne or Cadillac
Cheddar	England	Periquita, Zinfandel, Gewürztraminer *vendanges tardives*
Cheshire	England	Meursault, sweet white
Chèvre	France	Sancerre, Riesling, Crémant d'Alsace
Colby/Longhorn	Wisconsin	Zinfandel
Comté	Haute-Savoie, France	Chianti Classico Reserva, spicy white
Cornish Yarg	Cornwall, England	Mature red Bordeaux or Burgundy
Coulommiers	France	Côtes du Rhône, unoaked Chardonnay

CHEESE	REGION OF ORIGIN	WINE STYLE
Cream cheese	Everywhere	New World Pinot Noir
Crottin de Chavignol	Central France	Sancerre, Entre-Deux-Mers, Graves
Danish Blue	Denmark	Schnapps, Sauternes
Edam	Netherlands	Syrah, Zinfandel, Pauillac
Emmental	Switzerland	Côtes du Rhône, Shiraz
Epoisses	Burgundy	Mature red or white Burgundy
Esrom	Denmark	Valpolicella
Feta	Greece	Ouzo, Chardonnay
Fontina	Northwest Italy	Barbaresco
Fourme d'Ambert	Central France	Côtes du Rhône, Port, l'Etoile
Gaperon	Auvergne, France	Tokàji, vodka
Gjetost	Norway	Madeira, sweet white
Gloucester	England	Zinfandel
Gorgonzola	Northern Italy	Barolo, sweet white, Gigondas
Gouda	Netherlands	Chardonnay, white Burgundy, Chinon
Grana Padano	Northern Italy	Vino Nobile di Montepulciano
Gruyère	Switzerland	Bordeaux, Chasselas, Alsace Pinot Gris
Gubbeen	Southern Ireland	Oaky, mature white Burgundy
Havarti	Denmark	Light young red
Idiazabal	Northern Spain	White oaked Rioja
Kefalotiri	Greece	Bordeaux
Lanark Blue	Scotland	Sauternes
Lancashire	England	Burgundy, fresh Pinot Noir
Langres	France	Mature red Burgundy, Champagne
Leicester	England	Red Provence, full, rustic red
Limburg	Germany	Garrafeira red, Tokay Pinot Gris
Livarot	Normandy, France	Ste-Croix-du-Mont, Bonnezeaux
Mahon	Spain	Rioja
Manchego	Spain	Amontillado

CHEESE	REGION OF ORIGIN	WINE STYLE
Maroilles	France	Pacherenc du Vic-Bilh
Morbier	Jura, France	Arbois white, Gevrey-Chambertin
Monterey Jack	California	New World Chardonnay
Mozzarella	Italy	Chablis, Orvieto, Soave, Pinot Grigio
Muenster	Alsace, France	Gewürztraminer, Loupiac, Coteaux du Layon
Parmigiano-Reggiano	Northern Italy	Barolo, Barbaresco, Taurasi
Pont l'Evèque	Normandy, France	Mature red and white Burgundy, Bourgueil
Port Salut	Brittany, France	Bergerac, red Burgundy
Provolone	Italy	Young Chianti, Bardolino, Dolcetto d'Alba
Raclette	Switzerland	Chasselas, Chablis, Côtes de Duras
Reblochon	Savoie, France	Chardonnay, Crepy, Lirac, Sancerre
Robiola	Italy	Prosecco
Roquefort	France	Sauternes, Port, Châteauneuf-du-Pape, Vin de Paille
Ste-Maure	Loire, France	Chinon, Sancerre, Coteaux du Layon, Alsace Pinot Gris
St-Nectaire	Auvergne, France	Côtes du Rhône, Sancerre, Fronsac, Mâcon
Selles-sur-Cher	Central France	Sancerre, Romorantin, Reuilly
Shropshire Blue	England	Bordeaux, Cadillac
Stilton	England	Port, Sauternes, Ste-Croix-du-Mont
Taleggio	Italy	Soave, Chianti
Tête de Moine	Switzerland	Côtes du Rhône, mature white Burgundy
Tetilla	Spain	Cava
Tilsit	Germany	Gewürztraminer
Tomme de Savoie	France	Beaujolais, Varois
Vacherin Mont d'Or	Savoie, France	Tokay Pinot Gris, Chablis, Corton, Barsac

Fresh Fruit

Fruits that are high in acid can make wines taste metallic and thin. In general, drink sweet whites, especially botrytized, late-harvest, or sparkling wines. These are the best solutions for fruit, whether it be in a salad or as part of a dessert. Actually, sweet white wines and sparkling wines can take most meals from appetizers to dessert and coffee. Try it sometime.

Chocolate

Faced with such an aromatic prospect as chocolate, the task of finding a suitable wine seems daunting. A general rule, however, is that a good Port or Banyuls with most chocolate desserts, or chocolate alone, does well. With a very dark and strong chocolate, try a Mas Amiel (Maury). To accompany milk chocolate desserts or fruit and chocolate desserts, try a Gewürztraminer *vendanges tardives,* or a Muscat de Beaumes-de-Venise. Dry red wines such as a Bordeaux like St-Julien, or a Rasteau or Côtes du Rhône, can also work.

Some Classic Food and Wine Combinations

- Barbecued ribs with Zinfandel
- Beef stew or game casseroles with Barolo
- Brie with Meursault
- Caviar with Champagne
- Charcuterie with Beaujolais Cru
- Crottin de Chèvre with Sancerre
- Farmhouse Cheddar with sweet Jurançon
- Foie gras with Sauternes
- Seafood with Muscadet sur lie
- Ratatouille with Côtes de Provence rosé
- Roast spring lamb with Pauillac
- Roquefort with Sauternes
- Sole with white Burgundy
- St-Maure with Vouvray
- Stilton with vintage Port

REGIONAL PORTRAITS

Regional pairings are the most basic and understandable illustration of food and wine pairings. Here are three that showcase some of the most delicious wine and food pairings to appear on any table.

Alsace: Portrait of a Region

Alsace is a perfect French region in which to study food and wine matches, as it makes wine varietals, not blends. There is also a very strong regional cuisine.

Sylvaner

Fresh, fruity, and light, Sylvaner is ideal to accompany oysters and other shellfish, snails, fish, quiche lorraine, and delicatessen platters. It is heavenly with a *salade Vosgienne* (mushrooms, red potatoes, Muenster cheese, cumin, smoked lardons, croutons, and poached eggs), with their famous onion and béchamel sauce tart, or with *flammenküeche* (a thin, flat bread dough rectangle filled with lightly fried onions, cream, and smoked bacon).

Riesling

The pride of Alsace, with its delicate fruit and subtle bouquet, Riesling is perfect with fish, shellfish (especially lobster and crab), white meats, and, of course, *choucroute* (a dish of sauerkraut, boiled meats, and potatoes). Its perfect mate, however, is a *kougelhopf* (or savory brioche) of salmon and pike. *Kougelhopf* can, in fact, be either savory or sweet, but is always made in the shape of a large brioche.

Gewürztraminer

This noble, full-bodied, and structured nectar is ideal with exotic, spicy dishes and strong cheeses, as well as with desserts such as crème brûlée, or alone as an aperitif. Try it with a *brioche de foie gras* (duck pâté *en croûte*) instead of the usual Sauternes. It works beautifully with pork tenderloin in a sweet-and-sour sauce. And, of course, the local *grumbeerekiechle* (potato pancakes) with salmon and horseradish and their *tarte aux pommes à l'alsaciènne* (an apple tart with a ground almond filling).

Pinot Blanc

Fresh and supple, Pinot Blanc marries well with almost everything, but does better with fish, especially trout or sole with dill seed, and shellfish, particularly oysters.

Tokay Pinot Gris

A grape variety that fits in somewhere between the steely crispness of a Riesling and the sweeter opulence of a Gewürztraminer, it complements foie gras and most fowl (turkey, goose, *magret de canard*, sweetbreads in cream with morel mushrooms) and game (venison or wild boar). Also try it with mussels and lobster tails in a saffron and cream sauce. My favourite match is with *baeckaoffa* (a slow-cooked, marinated meat stew with onions, potatoes, and seasoning).

Pinot Noir

Not to be confused with the Burgundian style of Pinot Noir, here it is lighter (it is often a rosé) and fruitier. It goes very well with lamb and other red meats, delicatessen platters, and cheeses such as goat's cheese and Cheddar. Try it with gamier poultry with tarragon sauce or turkey stuffed with cèpes and minced veal and pork.

Crémant d'Alsace

Like Champagne, this goes with everything, although a heavy game dish might overpower it. Otherwise try it with foie gras or a sweet *kougelhopf*. This is often a better accompaniment than the heavy, classic Sauternes or Gewürztraminer. Then drink it throughout the rest of the meal with the seafood, cheese, dessert, and then, of course, continue long into the night!

A special treat, Clos de Zahnacker is the deliciously unique concoction of Riesling, Tokay Pinot Gris, and Gewürztraminer (produced by my good friends at the Caves de Ribeauvillé in Ribeauvillé) with a *presskopf* (a sort of terrine) of fresh wild salmon, lobster, and oysters in a creamy sauce of caviar, parsley, tarragon, and chives.

Provence: Portrait of a Region

Garlic, basil, olive oil, ripe plum tomatoes—delicious. Just mention the word *Provence* and my mouth waters. I think if I had to say that I learned to taste wines while living in Paris, it was living in Nice for a couple of years that taught me how to cook and eat, and seriously shop for fresh, quality ingredients.

There are eight AOC appellations in Provence: Côtes de Provence, Coteaux d'Aix-en-Provence, Coteaux d'Aix-en-Provence les Baux, Palette, Bandol, Cassis, Bellet, and the Coteaux Varois.

The reds and rosés are mostly composed of Mourvèdre (robust and aromatic), Grenache (full bodied and vital), Cinsault (fresh and fruity), Syrah (rich and spicy), Tibouren (fine and elegant), and Cabernet Sauvignon—apart from Bellet, which is principally of Braquet, Folle Noir, and Cinsault.

The whites are herby brews of Bourboulenc, Clairette, Ugni Blanc, Sauvignon Blanc, Marsanne, Rolle, and Sémillon. Their aromas vary from pears and lemons to roses and lavender with hints of exotic spices.

- *Légumes farcies* (meat-filled vegetables) with a rosé from Bandol or Bellet
- *Tapenade* (anchovy, garlic, and olive spread) with a fruity rosé
- *Anchoîade* (puree of anchovies, olive oil, and seasonal vegtables) with a light, fruity Côtes de Provence rosé
- *Pan bagna* (bread coated in olive oil, garlic, and tomatoes) with a red Côtes de Provence or Cassis
- *La tourte de blette* (a savory tart of chard leaves and zucchini) with an herby, substantial white Bandol
- *La bouillabaisse* (a medley of fish and seafood cooked in a sauce of white wine, olive oil, tomatoes, garlic, saffron, parsley, and herbs) with a Côtes de Provence rosé
- *Ravioli niçoise* (ravioli filled with the juice of *daube de boeuf*) with a red Bandol
- *La daube de boeuf* (beef braised in red wine and herb sauce) with a red Côtes de Provence or Coteaux d'Aix-en-Provence
- *Ratatouille niçoise* (onions, zucchini, eggplant, peppers, and tomatoes in olive oil and herbs) with Côtes de Provence rosé or white
- *Salade niçoise* (tomatoes, cucumber, broad beans, peppers, onion, eggs, anchovies, olives, olive oil, garlic, and basil) with rosés from Bellet, Palette, Cassis, or Bandol
- *Le socca* (a chickpea cake) with sweet and fruity rosés
- Crystallized fruits and *fougasse* (a fruitcakelike bread) with Muscat de Beaumes-de-Venise

Piedmont: Portrait of a Region

Barbaresco, Barolo, Barbera d'Alba, Barbera d'Asti, Boca, Bramaterra, Brachetto d'Acqui—bbbeautiful! Why is it that the names of most of my favorite Italian wines begin with the letter *B* and are from Piedmont? Bordering France and Switzerland, nestled at the foot of the Alps and the Apennines (hence its name: *piemonte*, or "foot of the mountain"), this region is only seventh among Italy's regions in terms of total production, but it has the most DOC and DOCG quality designation zones and the most vineyards dedicated to classified production.

Almost all of these classified wines are issued from indigenous grape varieties such as Nebbiolo, Barbera, Freisa, Grignolino, and Brachetto. They are elaborate, sensual, complex, stunning, sometimes fresh (Freisa), sometimes slightly acidic (Barbera), but, on the whole, thoroughly succulent wines. And they are perfect mates for the region's equally ample cuisine: game, buttery sauces, polenta, white truffle, risotto. Where else would you find a fondue dish served with two kinds of pasta, wheat based and potato based (gnocchi), in the same meal? My kind of country. For the more timid, Piedmont also has the fruity, gentle Dolcetto and an entire gamut of whites.

- *Salada di coconi* (mushroom salad with anchovies and hard-boiled eggs) with Asti Spumante or Barbera
- *Brasato al Barolo* (braised beef) with a Barolo, naturally
- *La bagna caoda* (anchovy dip with hot oil for vegetables) with a Freisa or a Barbera
- *Bollito* (boiled meats with spicy-hot sauces) with Barolo or Barbaresco
- *Fonduta* (melted Fontina cheese, butter, and eggs over polenta or pasta) with a Dolcetto, Barbera, or Barolo
- *Carbonata* (rich beef stew) with a Barolo
- *Vitello tonnato* (veal in a tuna and anchovy sauce) with Grignolino d'Asti or Dolcetto
- *Lepre in salmi Val d'Aosta* (hare casserole in Barbera) with a mature Barbera
- *Bunet Piemontese* (amaretto biscuit and egg custard pudding) with Asti Spumante

Wine and Food Pairing Rules

Here are a few simple rules to help you make the perfect matches with your food and wine.

- Match food and wine flavors: Herbal Sauvignon Blancs match vegetables; peppery Cabernet Sauvignons match steak in pepper sauce; buttery, oaky Chardonnays match fish and pasta in creamy sauces.
- Match food and wine textures: The sweet unctuousness of Sauternes matches foie gras; crisp, lively Sancerre matches oysters.
- Match food and wine weights: Again, Sauternes and foie gras match in richness; heavy Barolos match robust game dishes; light poached fish dishes match light dry wines.
- Always cook with wine that you would also drink, or drink the same wine that was used in the food's preparation.
- Learn and rely upon regional and local associations: Sancerre and Chavignol, for example.
- The new Pacific Rim and Mediterrasian cooking goes well with New World varietals.
- Follow the sauce of the dish and use its dominant flavor as your guide.
- Remember that opposites attract: Like sweet-and-sour sauce, a sweet wine balances an acidic or sour food.
- Strive for balance and respect between wine and food: An older, more complex wine takes center stage and should be served with very simple foods—not heavy sauces that will drown it.
- Remember that there are wine types that will go with just about everything, just as there are foods that will go with almost any wine, like roast chicken.
- Hard-to-match foods such as chocolate, strong cheeses, grapefruit, asparagus, and pickles should be teamed with the wines from the same region as the dish.
- Keep in mind the cooking method of the dish as well as the winemaking technique.
- Match the wine to the occasion and environment as well as the food: picnic? beach? work dinner?
- Rule Number One: When in doubt, drink Champagne!

PART 3

WINES
AND
FOODS

The following food and wine cross-reference list is not meant to be all-encompassing. Indeed, such a feat would be beside the point, as the idea is not to create a gustatory dictate or dictionary, but rather a guide to pleasurable frolicking for your taste buds.

The foods and wines listed are an odd mix from the very general to the very specific, hoping to capture larger flavor groups as well as more specific and illustrative examples. These matches are a smattering of ideas meant to get your own taste buds activated and to be used to invent your own taste pairings. Do not consider the suggestions to be exhaustive or inflexible—just because Chilean Chardonnay is matched to carrot soup does not mean that this is the only Chardonnay that will do. I have used it as an example either because I personally find a certain *je ne sais quoi* in the combination, or because I am trying to represent equally the geographical distribution of the world's Chardonnay production.

I have included some wines that may be more expensive or more difficult to find if I felt that they were the very best example I could give, but all the wines listed are available in the United States. If you do find that the wine listed is too expensive or hard to come by, you can buy the New World version for everyday and save the real thing for special occasions. "Why so much detail to specific wines?" I hear you ask. Well, if when cooking your Sunday roast you choose your spices, gravy, and vegetables with care, then the natural evolution is to include the wine in the equation in the same way. Consider the wine as something on your plate and not in the glass, next to the plate—it is part of the meal, not an adjunct.

There are enough wines listed to be able to extrapolate a taste theme. When the European wines are cited, you can use the Which Grapes Make Which Wines? table on page 28 to find New World grape variety substitutes. For example, the Rhône Valley's Condrieu is produced from the white grape variety Viognier, so you can eat your ceviche just as pleasurably with a Viognier grown elsewhere—variations on its theme are assumed and permitted.

Old World appellation and vineyard subtleties are slightly bowed to, yet it would be a bit too restrictive to insist that only a Gevrey-Chambertin could do the trick and that a Chambertin just couldn't possibly. There are also references to a wine's classification, such as Villages, Premier Cru, or Grand Cru. As you move up to the next quality classification, you are looking for a more serious version bearing greater weight and concentration, which is a result of the more attentive viticultural and vinicultural practices (such as lower yields, less oak, and so on, as discussed in part 1).

When discussing varietals such as Chardonnay and Cabernet Sauvignon, the term *New World* is used to signify that most exported versions of a particular European variety will do very nicely in that particular case. To be honest, I find the nuances among the New World exports becoming less significant, as "clean" winemaking techniques are still in international vogue. Just note that most New World versions tend to taste oakier, sweeter, and monolithic, whereas their Old World counterparts are more subtle, dry, and complex, becoming more opulent with age. Hence the New World wines match the bold, spicy New World cuisine, and the Old World wines are best with their corresponding regional cuisines. Although this is not to say that European wine and food lacks boldness and spice—don't confuse *subtle* with *boring!*

Finally, these culinary couplings are a mixture of the tried and true as well as those from years of my tasting notes gleaned from the back of lipstick-stained dinner napkins. I know that it is hard to please all of the people all of the time, and I would be quite happy to please somebody just once. In that light, I supplied, if applicable, wines for each food entry that were New World and Old World, sweet and dry, red, white, and rosé. I did not always list and match all of a wine's types. For example, I mention red Dão but not white. However, if you refer to the Which Grapes Make Which Wines? chart, you will find a complete listing of wine styles.

The second half of this listing, the wine to food section, was tricky, as there are many more dishes for each wine than there are wines for each dish—so again, for space and clarity, the wine guide is not exhaustive. The point of the exercise is not to tell you what and how to eat and drink, but to provide a quick and easy guide as well as to present a springboard of ideas for your own adventures.

Bon appètit!

 FOOD TO WINE INDEX

FOOD	WINE NAME	REGION/ COUNTRY	WINE STYLE
AIOLI	Bordeaux rosé	Bordeaux	dry rosé
	Palette	Provence	dry rosé
	Soave	Italy	dry white
ALMONDS, grilled and salted	Chablis	Burgundy	dry white
	Fino Sherry	Spain	fortified white
	Moscatel de Setúbal	Portugal	sweet white
ANCHOVY/ ANCHOVY PASTE	Bandol	Provence	dry rosé
	Fino Sherry	Spain	fortified white
	Greco di Tufo	Italy	dry white
	Saumur	Loire	dry white
	Sylvaner	Alsace	dry white
	Tavel	Rhône	dry rosé

FOOD	WINE NAME	REGION/ COUNTRY	WINE STYLE
ANDOUILLETTE,	Arbois	Jura	dry white
GRILLED WITH	Grenache	France or NW	dry red
MUSTARD	Minervois	Languedoc-	
		Roussillon	dry red
	Palette	Provence	dry red
ANTIPASTI	Bardolino	Italy	dry red
	Dolcetto d'Alba	Italy	dry white
	Falerno del Massico	Italy	dry white
	Verdicchio	Italy	dry white

APPLE PIE (see DESSERTS with a base of APPLES)

FOOD	WINE NAME	REGION/ COUNTRY	WINE STYLE
ARTICHOKES	Chardonnay (unoaked)	Burgundy or NW	dry white
	Rully	Burgundy	dry white
	Sauvignon Blanc	New Zealand	dry white
	Viognier	Rhône or NW	dry white
ASPARAGUS	Bourgueil or Chinon	Loire	dry red
	Gewürztraminer	Alsace	dry white
	Muscat (dry)	Alsace	dry white
	Sauvignon Blanc	New Zealand	dry white
ASPARAGUS IN	L'Etoile	Jura	dry white
CREAM SAUCE	Meursault	Burgundy	dry white
	Muscat	Alsace	dry white
	Petit Chablis	Burgundy	dry white
ASPARAGUS IN	Côtes du St-Mont	Southwest France	dry white
VINAIGRETTE	St-Véran	Burgundy	dry white
SAUCE	Tavel	Rhône	dry rosé
AVOCADO	Chablis	Burgundy	dry white
	Champagne (brut)	Champagne	sparkling
	Sancerre	Loire/Centre	dry white
	Sauvignon Blanc	New Zealand	dry white
BACLAVA	Beaumes-de-Venise	Rhône	vin doux naturel
	Moscatel du Setúbal	Portugal	sweet white
	Samos	Greece	sweet white
BACON	Beaujolais	Burgundy	dry red
	Chardonnay	Burgundy or NW	dry white
	Pinot Noir	New World	dry red

FOOD	WINE NAME	REGION/ COUNTRY	WINE STYLE
BAGELS WITH	Chablis	Burgundy	dry white
SALMON AND	Champagne (brut)	Champagne	sparkling
CREAM CHEESE	Pinot Noir	Romania	dry red
BAKED BEANS	Bourgueil	Loire	dry red
	Cabernet Franc	New World	dry red
	Zinfandel	California	dry red

BANANAS (see DESSERTS with a base of BANANAS)

BARBECUED	Cinsault	Lebanon	dry red
MEATS	Gewürztraminer	Alsace	dry white
	Lirac	Rhône	dry red
	Mourvèdre	France	dry red
	Shiraz	Australia	dry red
	Zinfandel	California	dry red
BARBECUED	Bordeaux Sec	Bordeaux	dry white
FISH	Entre-Deux-Mers	Bordeaux	dry white
	Sémillon	Australia	dry white
BASS,	Chardonnay	France or NW	dry white
grilled	Pouilly-Fuissé	Burgundy	dry white
	Tocia Friulano Collio	Italy	dry white
BEAN AND	Bergerac	Southwest France	dry red
PASTA SOUP	Buzet	Southwest France	dry red
	Côte Rôtie	Rhône	dry red
	Shiraz	Australia	dry red

BEAUFORT (see CHEESE AND WINE on page 87)

BEEF	Barolo	Italy	dry red
	Corbières	Languedoc	dry red
	Gigondas	Rhône	dry red
	Juliénas	Beaujolais	dry red
	Pomerol	Bordeaux	dry red
BEEF	Rioja	Spain	dry red
POTPIE	St-Emilion	Bordeaux	dry red
	Zinfandel	California	dry red

FOOD	WINE NAME	REGION/ COUNTRY	WINE STYLE
BEEF	Barolo	Italy	dry red
BOURGUIGNONNE	Brouilly	Beaujolais	dry red
	Clos de Vougeot	Burgundy	dry red
	Gigondas	Rhône	dry red
	Kékfrankos	Hungary	dry red
	Saumur	Loire	dry red
BEEF SIRLOIN	Cabernet Sauvignon	California	dry red
WITH	Chinon	Loire	dry red
MUSHROOMS	Mercurey	Burgundy	dry red
	Merlot	New World	dry red
	Pomerol	Bordeaux	dry red
BEEF	Bordeaux rosé	Bordeaux	dry rosé
STROGANOFF	Kékfrankos	Hungary	dry red
	Mavrud	Bulgaria	dry red
	Merlot	New World	dry red
	Meursault	Burgundy	dry white
	Vacqueyras	Rhône	dry red
BEEF TACOS	Zinfandel	California	dry red
	Riesling	NW or Alsace	dry white
BEEF	Champagne (brut)	Champagne	sparkling
WELLINGTON	St-Emilion	Bordeaux	dry red
	Malbec	Argentina	dry red
	Merlot	New World	dry red
BLACKENED	Chardonnay	Chile	dry white
FISH	Entre-Deux-Mers	Bordeaux	dry white
	Sémillon	Australia	dry white
BLANQUETTE	Côtes de Provence	Provence	dry rosé
DE VEAU	Minervois	Languedoc-Roussillon	dry rosé
	Muscadet	Loire	dry white
	Riesling Grand Cru	Alsace	dry white

BLEU d'AUVERGNE (see CHEESE AND WINE on page 87)

BLINIS WITH	Champagne	Champagne	sparkling
TARAMA or SALMON	Crémant de Bourgogne	Burgundy	sparkling
BLUE CHEESE	Aligoté	Burgundy	dry white
DIP	Cadillac	Bordeaux	sweet white
	Champagne	Champagne	sparkling

FOOD	WINE NAME	REGION/ COUNTRY	WINE STYLE
BOAR (see WILD BOAR)			
BOEUF	Bandol	Provence	dry red
EN DAUBE	Barolo	Italy	dry red
	Hermitage	Rhône	dry red
	Shiraz	Australia	dry red
	Vin de Corse	Corsica	dry red
BORSCHT	Chianti	Italy	dry red
	Copertino	Italy	dry red
	Kékfrankos	Hungary	dry red
BOUILLABAISSE	Riesling	Alsace	dry white
	Tavel	Provence	dry rosé
	Vin de Corse	Corsica	dry white
BRESCIOLA	Chianti	Italy	dry red
	Sangiovese	California	dry red
	Valpolicella	Italy	dry red
BRIE (see CHEESE AND WINE on page 87)			
BROWN SUGAR (as a principal ingredient or dominant flavor)			
	Gewürztraminer	Alsace	sweet white
	Riesling Auslese	Germany	sweet white
	Sauternes	Bordeax	sweet white
	Vosne-Romanée	Burgundy	dry red
BROWNIES (see DESSERTS with a base of CHOCOLATE)			
BRUNSWICK	Bergerac	Southwest France	dry red
STEW	St-Véran/Mâcon	Burgundy	dry white
	Zinfandel	California	dry white
BRUSCHETTA	Chardonnay	Chile	dry white
	Soave	Italy	dry white
	Vernaccia di San Gimignano	Italy	dry white
BRUSSELS	Arbois	Jura	dry white
SPROUTS	Côtes de Provence	Provence	dry red
	Pinot Noir	New World	dry red
BUFFALO	Buzet	Southwest France	dry red
WINGS	Côtes du Roussillon	Roussillon	dry red
	Zinfandel	California	dry red

FOOD	WINE NAME	REGION/ COUNTRY	WINE STYLE
CABBAGE,	Bourgueil	Loire	dry red
stuffed	Crozes-Hermitage	Rhône	dry red
	Shiraz	Australia	dry red

CABICHOU (see CHEESE AND WINE on page 87)

CAESAR SALAD (see SALADS)

CAJUN-STYLE	Pommard	Burgundy	dry red
MEATS	Syrah	New World	dry red
	Zinfandel	California	dry red

CALAMARI (see SQUID)

CAMEMBERT (see CHEESE AND WINE on page 87)

CARP, grilled (see also FISH or SEAFOOD)

	Pouilly-Fumé	Loire	dry white
	Sauvignon Blanc	New World	dry white
	Ugni Blanc	New World	dry white
	Trebbiano	Italy	dry white

CARPACCIO	Champagne rosé	Champagne	sparkling
	Chianti	Italy	dry red
	Reguengos	Portugal	dry red
	Sangiovese	California	dry red

| CARROT CAKE | Crémant de Bourgogne | Burgundy | sparkling |
| | Tokàji | Hungary | sweet white |

CARROT SOUP	Chablis Grand Cru	Burgundy	dry white
	Chardonnay	Chile	dry white
	Viognier	Italy	dry white

CASSOULET	Barbaresco	Italy	dry red
	Cahors	Southwest France	dry red
	Corbières	Languedoc	dry red
	Mourvèdre	France or NW	dry red
	Shiraz	Australia	dry red
	Zinfandel	California	dry red

CAVIAR	Champagne NV	Champagne	sparkling
	Châteauneuf-du-Pape	Rhône	dry white
	Puligny-Montrachet	Burgundy	dry white
	Pinot Gris	Alsace	dry white

FOOD	WINE NAME	REGION/ COUNTRY	WINE STYLE
CEVICHE	Condrieu	Rhône	dry white
	Ribeiro	Spain	dry white
	Sauvignon Blanc	Chile	dry white
	Vinho Verde	Portugal	dry white
CHARCUTERIE	Bardolino	Italy	dry red
	Beaujolais	Burgundy	dry red
	Cabernet Sauvignon	Chile	dry red
	Chinon	Loire	dry red
	Côtes du Rhône	Rhône	dry red
	Rully	Burgundy	dry red
CHATEAUBRIAND	Margaux	Bordeaux	dry red
	Barolo	Italy	dry red
	Echezeaux	Burgundy	dry red
CHEESE (see CHEESE AND WINE on page 87)			
CHEESECAKE	Cadillac	Bordeaux	sweet white
	Champagne	Champagne	sparkling
	Coteaux du Layon	Loire	sweet white
	Monbazillac	Bordeaux	sweet white
	Pacherenc du Vic-Bilh	Southwest France	sweet white
CHEF'S SALAD (see SALADS)			
CHICKEN, plain roast	Bergerac	Southwest France	dry red
	Bordeaux Supérieur	Bordeaux	dry red
	Chardonnay (oaked)	Chile or NW	dry white
	Gamay	Beaujolais, Burgundy	dry red
	Pinot Noir	New World	dry red
CHICKEN, BASQUE	Châteauneuf-du-Pape	Rhône	dry red
	Corbières	Languedoc	dry red
	Fronsac	Bordeaux	dry red
CHICKEN, CREOLE	Gewürztraminer	Alsace	dry white
	Sancerre	Loire/Centre	dry white
	Sauvignon Blanc	New Zealand	dry white
	Savennières	Loire	dry white

FOOD	WINE NAME	REGION/ COUNTRY	WINE STYLE
CHICKEN,	Arbois	Jura	dry white
CURRY	Chardonnay	New World	dry white
	Côtes du Rhône	Rhône	dry red
	Morgon	Beaujolais	dry red
	Pinot Gris	Alsace	dry white
	St-Emilion	Bordeaux	dry red
CHICKEN,	Champagne rosé	Champagne	sparkling
LEMON	Chenin Blanc	Loire or NW	dry white
	Saumur Champigny	Loire	dry red
CHICKEN	Chablis Premier Cru	Burgundy	dry white
in MOREL	Chardonnay	New World	dry white
and CREAM	Corbières	Languedoc	dry white
SAUCE	Pinot Noir	Oregon, USA	dry red
	Riesling	Alsace	dry white
CHICKEN,	Kékfrankos	Hungary	dry red
PAPRIKA	Shiraz	Australia	dry red
	Zinfandel	California	dry red
CHICKEN	Periquita	Portugal	dry red
PIRI-PIRI	Renguengos	Portugal	dry red
	Sauvignon Blanc	New World	dry white
	Vinho Verde	Portugal	dry white
CHICKEN,	Bourgueil	Loire	dry red
SAUCE CHASSEUR	Entre-Deux-Mers	Bordeaux	dry white
	Médoc	Bordeaux	dry red
	Savigny-Les-Beaune	Burgundy	dry red
	Sémillon	California	dry white
CHICKEN,	Bordeaux Supérieur	Bordeaux	dry red
SOUTHERN	Buzet	Southwest France	dry red
FRIED	Shiraz	Australia	dry red
CHICKEN,	Gewürztraminer VT	Alsace	dry to medium-sweet white
SWEET-and-			
SOUR SAUCE	Pomerol	Bordeaux	dry red
	Muscat de Rivesaltes	Roussillon	dry red
	Sylvaner	Alsace	dry white

FOOD	WINE NAME	REGION/ COUNTRY	WINE STYLE
CHICKEN TAGINE (see COUSCOUS)			
CHICKEN, TARRAGON	Cahors	Southwest France	dry red
	Crozes-Hermitage	Rhône	dry red
	Mourvèdre	New World	dry red
	Savigny-Les-Beaune	Burgundy	dry red
CHICKEN TERIYAKI	Sancerre	Loire/Centre	dry white
	Sauvignon Blanc	New Zealand	dry white
	Soave	Italy	dry white
CHICKEN TIKKA MASALA (see INDIAN FOOD)			
CHICKEN TETRAZZINI	Chardonnay (oaked)	New World	dry white
	Côtes Chalonnaise	Burgundy	dry white
	Rully	Burgundy	dry white
CHILI CON CARNE	Cabernet Sauvignon	Argentina or Chile	dry red
	Côtes du Rhône	Rhône	dry red
	Pinotage	South Africa	dry red
	Shiraz	Australia	dry red
	Zinfandel	California	dry red
CHINESE FOOD	Riesling VT	Alsace	dry to medium-sweet white
	Riesling Spätlese	Germany	dry to medium-sweet white
	Gewürztraminer VT	Alsace	dry to medium-sweet white
	Champagne NV	Champagne	sparkling
	Chasselas	Switzerland	dry white
	Grüner Veltliner BA	Austria	sweet white
CHORIZO	Corbières	Languedoc	dry red
	Irouléguy	Southwest France	dry red
	Navarra	Spain	dry red
	Pinotage	South Africa	dry red
	Zinfandel	California	dry red
CHOUCROUTE GARNI	Chablis (unoaked)	Burgundy	dry white
	Crozes-Hermitage	Rhône	dry white
	Pinot Blanc	Alsace	dry white
	Riesling	Germany	dry white

FOOD	WINE NAME	REGION/ COUNTRY	WINE STYLE
CHUTNEY (see INDIAN FOOD)			
CLAM CHOWDER	Chablis Grand Cru	Burgundy	dry white
	Chardonnay	Long Island	dry white
	L'Etoile	Jura	dry white
	Riesling	Alsace	dry white
	Pinot Gris	Alsace	dry white
COD, salt, with garlic, oil, and cream (see also FISH or SEAFOOD)			
	Côtes de Provence	Provence	dry rosé
	Mâcon	Burgundy	dry white
	Sylvaner	Alsace	dry white
CONFIT	Cahors	Southwest France	dry red
DU CANARD	Merlot	New World	dry red
	Pommard	Burgundy	dry red
	St-Emilion	Bordeaux	dry red
	Saumur	Loire	dry red
COQ AU VIN	Châteauneuf-du-Pape	Rhône	dry red
	Corbières	Languedoc	dry red
	Côtes du Rhône	Rhône	dry red
	Gevrey-Chambertin	Burgundy	dry red
	Pinot Noir	California	dry red
COQUILLES ST-JACQUES (see SCALLOPS)			
CORN BREAD	Chardonnay	New World	dry white
	Côtes du Jura	Jura	dry red
	Merlot	New World	dry red
	Vin de Corse	Corsica	dry red
CORN CHOWDER	Chardonnay	California	dry white
	Meursault	Burgundy	dry white
CORN ON	Chardonnay	California	dry white
THE COB	Pinot Gris	Alsace	dry white
COULOMMIERS (see CHEESE AND WINE on page 87)			
COUSCOUS	Cabernet Sauvignon/		
	Cinsault	Lebanon	dry red
	Navarra	Spain	dry red
	Pinotage	South Africa	dry red
	Shiraz	Australia	dry red

FOOD	WINE NAME	REGION/ COUNTRY	WINE STYLE
CRAB	Chablis	Burgundy	dry white
	Crepy	Savoie	dry white
	Crozes-Hermitage	Rhône	dry white
	Entre-Deux-Mers	Bordeaux	dry white
	Muscadet	Loire	dry white
CREME CARAMEL/	Ausbrach	Austria	sweet white
BRULEE	Champagne, demi-sec	Champagne	sparkling
	Gaillac	Southwest France	dry white
	Sauternes	Bordeaux	sweet white
CREPES,	Alto Adige Chardonnay	Italy	dry white
SAVORY	Bordeaux Supérieur	Bordeaux	dry red
	Pinot Blanc	Alsace	dry white
	Rully	Burgundy	dry white
	St-Amour	Beaujolais	dry red
CREPES,	Champagne, demi-sec	Champgne	sparkling
SWEET	Vin de Paille	Jura	vin doux naturel
	Vouvray	Loire	sparkling (mousseux)
CROQUE	Anjou Gamay	Loire	dry red
MONSIEUR/	Bordeaux	Bordeaux	dry red
MADAME	Chardonnay	Australian	dry white
	Sylvaner	Alsace	dry white

CROTIN DE CHAVIGNOL (see CHEESE AND WINE on page 87)

FOOD	WINE NAME	REGION/ COUNTRY	WINE STYLE
CRUDITES	Gros Plant	Loire/Nantes	dry white
	Pinot Blanc	Alsace	dry white
	Pinot Grigio	Italy	dry white
CURRY	Condrieu	Rhône	dry white
(see also	Marsanne	New World	dry white
INDIAN FOOD)	Viognier	Rhône	dry white
CURRIED	Crozes-Hermitage	Rhône	dry white
TOMATO SOUP	Gewürztraminer	Alsace	dry white
	Marsanne	New World	dry white
	Rioja Reserva	Spain	dry red

DESSERTS with a base of APPLES

FOOD	WINE NAME	REGION/ COUNTRY	WINE STYLE
	Pineau de Charentes	Cognac	vin de liqueur
	Vin de Paille	Jura	vin doux naturel
	Vouvray	Loire	sweet white

FOOD	WINE NAME	REGION/ COUNTRY	WINE STYLE
DESSERTS with a base of APRICOTS			
	Aubruch	Austria	sweet white
	Blanquette de Limoux	Languedoc	sparkling
	Coteaux du Layon	Loire	sweet white
	Muscat de Rivesaltes	Roussillon	*vin doux naturel*
	Vin de Paille	Jura	*vin doux naturel*
DESSERTS with a base of BANANAS			
	Beaumes-de-Venise	Rhône	*vin doux naturel*
	Crémant de Bourgogne	Burgundy	sparkling
	Monbazillac	Bordeaux	sweet white
DESSERTS with a base of CARAMEL			
	Barsac	Bordeaux	sweet white
	Champagne (demi-sec)	Champagne	sparkling
	Moscatel de Setúbal	Portugal	sweet white
DESSERTS with a base of CASSIS			
	Bergerac	Southwest France	dry white
	Champagne rosé	Champagne	sparkling
	Muscat de Rivesaltes	Roussillon	*vin doux naturel*
DESSERTS with a base of CHERRIES			
	Black Muscat	California	sweet white
	Blanquette de Limoux	Languedoc	sparkling
	Coteaux du Layon	Loire	sweet white
	Riesling Beerenauslese	Germany	sweet white
DESSERTS with a base of CHESTNUTS			
	Asti Spumante	Italy	sparkling
	Chenin Blanc	Loire	dry white
	Loupiac	Bordeaux	sweet white
DESSERTS with a base of CHOCOLATE			
	Banyuls	Roussillon	*vin doux naturel*
	Champagne (Noir de Noirs)	Champagne	sparkling
	Moscatel de Setúbal	Portugal	sweet white
	Pineau de Charentes	Cognac	*vin de liqueur*
	Port	Portugal	fortified red
	Sauternes	Bordeaux	sweet white

FOOD	WINE NAME	REGION/ COUNTRY	WINE STYLE
DESSERTS with a base of COFFEE			
	Banyuls	Roussillon	*vin de liqueur* red
	Champagne (brut)	Champagne	sparkling
	Richebourg	Burgundy	dry red
	Vosne-Romanée	Burgundy	dry red
DESSERTS with a base of COGNAC			
	Arbois	Jura	dry white
	Pineau de Charentes	Cognac	*vin de liqueur* white
DESSERTS with a base of COINTREAU			
	Champagne	Champagne	sparkling
	Sauternes	Bordeaux	sweet white
DESSERTS with a base of FRUIT			
	Asti Spumante	Italy	sparkling
	Barsac/Sauternes	Bordeaux	sweet white
	Beaumes-de-Venise	Rhône	*vin doux naturel*
	Champagne (Blanc de Blancs)	Champagne	sparkling
	Coteaux du Layon	Loire	sweet white
	Monbazillac/Loupiac	Bordeaux	sweet white
	Quarts de Chaume	Loire	sweet white
	Vouvray	Loire	sweet white
DESSERTS with a base of GINGER			
	Beaumes-de-Venise	Rhône	*vin doux naturel*
	Muscat	France	sweet white
	Sauvignon Blanc	France or NW	dry white
DESSERTS with a base of LEMON			
	Hermitage	Rhône	dry white
	Sauternes	Bordeaux	sweet white
	Vouvray	Loire	sweet white
DESSERTS with a base of MINT			
	Asti Spumante	Italy	sparkling
	Beaumes-de-Venise	Rhône	*vin doux naturel*
DESSERTS with a base of ORANGE			
	Muscat de Rivesaltes	Rhône	sweet white
	Ste-Croix-du-Mont	Southwest France	sweet white

FOOD	WINE NAME	REGION/ COUNTRY	WINE STYLE
DESSERTS with a base of PINEAPPLE			
	Cadillac	Bordeaux	sweet white
	Champagne (demi-sec)	Champagne	sparkling
	Muscat de Rivesaltes	Roussillon	*vin doux naturel*
	Pacherenc du Vic-Bilh	Southwest France	dry to sweet white
DESSERTS with a base of RASPBERRIES			
	Beaujolais-Villages	Beaujolais	dry red
	Champagne (demi-sec)	Champagne	sparkling
	Coteaux du Layon	Loire	sweet white
	Loupiac	Bordeaux	sweet white
	Riesling	Alsace	dry white
	Saumur-Champigny	Loire	dry red
DESSERTS with a base of STRAWBERRIES			
	Banyuls	Roussillon	red
	Champagne	Champagne	sparkling
	Monbazillac	Bordeaux	sweet white
	Saumur-Champigny	Loire	dry red
DUCK, roast			
	Bonnes-Mares	Burgundy	dry red
	Châteauneuf-du-Pape	Rhône	dry red
	Madiran	Southwest France	dry red
	Pomerol	Bordeaux	dry red
	Pommard	Burgundy	dry red
	Zinfandel	California	dry red
DUCK à l'ORANGE	Cahors	Southwest France	dry red
	Côtes de Provence	Provence	dry red
	Gewürztraminer	Alsace	dry to medium- sweet white
	Graves	Bordeaux	dry red
	Riesling Auslese	Germany	sweet white
	Rosso Cònero	Italy	dry red
	Shiraz	Australia	dry red
DUCK LIVER (see FOIE GRAS)			
EELS, smoked	Bourgueil	Loire	dry red
	Sancerre	Loire	dry white
	Sauvignon Blanc	New Zealand	dry white

FOOD	WINE NAME	REGION/ COUNTRY	WINE STYLE
EELS,	Pouilly-Fumé	Loire	dry white
with a creamy	Riesling	Alsace	dry white
herb sauce	Sancerre	Loire/Centre	dry white
EGGPLANT	Corbières	Languedoc	dry red
	Dão	Portugal	dry red
	Vin de Corse	Corsica	dry red
	Zinfandel	California	dry red
EGGS	Brouilly	Burgundy	dry red
	Muscadet	Loire	dry white
	Sauvignon Blanc	France	dry white
EGGS, scrambled, with smoked salmon			
	Cava	Spain	sparkling
	Champagne rosé	Champagne	sparkling
	Chardonnay	Chile	dry white
	Petit Chablis	Burgundy	dry white
EGGS	Champagne	Champagne	sparkling
BENEDICT	Chardonnay (unoaked)	New World	dry white
	Pinot Blanc	Alsace	dry white
EMPANADAS	Malbec	Argentina	dry red
	Merlot	Chile	dry red
	Zinfandel	California	dry red
ESCARGOTS à la BOURGUIGNONNE			
	Aligoté	Burgundy	dry white
	Bourgueil	Loire	dry red
	Chablis	Burgundy	dry white
	Champagne (Blanc de Blancs)	Champagne	sparkling
	Côtes du Roussillon	Roussillon	dry red
	Vacqueyras	Rhône	dry red
FETTUCCINE ALFREDO			
	Alto Adige Chardonnay	Italy	dry white
	Frascati Superiore	Italy	dry white
FISH (see also specific types)			

FOOD	WINE NAME	REGION/ COUNTRY	WINE STYLE
FISH	Chardonnay (oaked)	California	dry white
(white)	Muscadet sur lie	Loire	dry white
	Sauvignon Blanc	New World	dry white
	Vouvray	Loire	dry white
FISH	Bergerac	Southwest France	dry red
(fried)	Pinot Grigio	Italy	dry white
	Verdicchio	Italy	dry white
FISH	Chenin Blanc	New World	dry white
(grilled)	Riesling	Alsace	dry white
FISH	Riesling Auslese	Germany	sweet white
(smoked)	Gewürztraminer VT	Alsace	sweet white
FISH AND	Bandol rosé	Côtes de Provence	dry rosé
CHIPS	Bergerac	Southwest France	dry white
	Mâcon or Rully	Burgundy	dry white
	Pinot Grigio	Italy	dry white
	Sauvignon Blanc	Chile	dry white
	Verdicchio	Italy	dry white
FISHCAKES	Chardonnay	Chile	dry white
	Muscadet	Loire	dry white
	Sancerre	Loire/Centre	dry white
	Sauvignon Blanc	New Zealand	dry white
FISH in	Barbaresco	Italy	dry red
RED WINE	Graves	Bordeaux	dry red
FOIE GRAS	Champagne		
	(Blanc de Blancs)	Champagne	sparkling
	Corton Charlemagne	Burgundy	dry white
	Monbazillac	Bordeaux	sweet white
	Pineau de Charentes	Cognac	vin de liqueur white
	Pinot Gris VY	Alsace	dry to medium-sweet white
	Riesling Auslese	Germany	sweet white
	Sauternes/Barsac	Bordeaux	sweet white
	Vin de Paille	Jura	sweet white

FOOD	WINE NAME	REGION/ COUNTRY	WINE STYLE
FONDUE, cheese (Savoyarde)			
	Chardonnay	California	dry white
	Chasselas	Switzerland or Alsace	dry white
	Côtes du Rhône	Rhône	dry red
	Mâcon	Burgundy	dry white
	Patrimonio	Corsica	dry white
	Varois	Switzerland	dry red
FONDUE, meat (Bourguignonne)			
	Bordeaux	Bordeaux	dry red
	Côte de Beaune	Burgundy	dry red
	Côtes du Rhône	Rhône	dry red
	Saumur	Loire	dry white
	Shiraz	Australia	dry red
FRUIT COMPOTE/SALAD (also see DESSERTS with a base of FRUIT)			
	Muscat de Rivesaltes	Roussillon	*vin doux naturel*
	Muscato Spumante	Italy	sparkling
	Loupiac	Bordeaux	sweet white
	Champagne rosé	Champagne	sparkling
GAME (see also specific types)			
	Barolo	Italy	dry red
	Bonnes-Mares	Burgundy	dry red
	Clos de Vougeot	Burgundy	dry red
	Corton	Burgundy	dry red
	Echezeaux	Burgundy	dry red
	Shiraz	Australia	dry red
	Syrah	New World	dry red
	Vosne-Romanée	Burgundy	dry red
GAZPACHO	Buzet	Southwest France	dry red
	Sauvignon Blanc	New Zealand	dry white
	Soave	Italy	dry white
	St-Georges-St-Emilion	Bordeaux	dry red
	Viognier	New World	dry white
GOOSE, stuffed with PRUNES or other FRUIT			
	Champagne	Champagne	dry sparkling
	Châteauneuf-du-Pape	Rhône	dry red
	Chianti Classico	Italy	dry red
	Gigondas	Rhône	dry red
	Margaux	Bordeaux	dry red

FOOD	WINE NAME	REGION/ COUNTRY	WINE STYLE
GOOSE, stuffed with PRUNES or other FRUIT *(continued)*			
	Pacherenc du Vic-Bilh	Southwest France	dry to sweet white
	Pomerol	Bordeaux	dry red
	Shiraz	Australia	dry red
	Vouvray	Loire, France	demi-sec white
GOUGERE	Chablis/Pouilly-Fuissé	Burgundy	dry white
	Côtes du Rhône	Rhône	dry red
	Pinot Gris	Alsace	dry white
GOULASH	Gigondas	Rhône	dry red
	Mavrud	Bulgaria	dry red
	Penedès	Spain	dry red
	Zinfandel	California	dry red
GRAVLAX	Champagne (Blanc de Blancs)	Champagne	sparkling
	Chardonnay	Australia	dry white
	Riesling Kabinett	Germany	dry white
GREEK FOOD	Naoussa	Greece	dry red
	Rioja	Spain	dry red
	Shiraz	Australia	dry red
	Zinfandel	California	dry red
GROUSE	Barolo	Italy	dry red
	Chambertin	Burgundy	dry red
	Hermitage	Rhône	dry red
	Richebourg	Burgundy	dry red
GUACAMOLE	Champagne	Champagne	sparkling
	Chardonnay	California	dry white
	Meursault	Burgundy	dry white
	Pinot Grigio	Italy	dry white
GUINEA HEN	Chambertin	Burgundy	dry red
	Fronsac	Bordeaux	dry red
	Pauillac	Bordeaux	dry red
HADDOCK	Arbois	Jura	dry red
	Graves	Bordeaux	dry white
	Riesling	Alsace	dry white
	Sauvignon Blanc	New World	dry white

FOOD	WINE NAME	REGION/ COUNTRY	WINE STYLE
HAM, BAKED WITH PINEAPPLES	Bourgueil	Loire, France	dry red
	Côtes de Montravel	Southwest France	dry white
	Saumur	Loire, France	medium-dry white
HAM, BAKED	Beaujolais	Burgundy	dry red
	Chinon	Loire	dry red
	Pinot Noir	New World	dry red
HAM, SMOKED	Pacherenc du Vic-Bilh	Southwest France	sweet white
	Riesling Spätlese	Germany	sweet white
	Riesling VT	Alsace	sweet white
HAMBURGERS	Beaujolais	Burgundy	dry red
	Cabernet Sauvignon	California	dry red
	Chianti	Italy	dry red
	Shiraz	Australia	dry red
	Zinfandel	California	dry red
HERBS and SPICES (see PART 2)			
HERRING	Corbières	Languedoc	dry white
	Entre-Deux-Mers	Bordeaux	dry white
	St-Véran	Burgundy	dry white
HUMMUS	Furmint	Hungary	dry white
	Pinot Grigio	Italy	dry white
	Zitsa	Greece	dry white
ICE CREAM	Beaumes-de-Venise	Rhône	vin doux naturel
	Champagne	Champagne	sparkling
	Muscat	France	sweet white
	Passito	Italy	sweet white
INDIAN FOOD WITH SPICY YOGURT SAUCES			
	Bordeaux rosé	Bordeaux	dry rosé
	Champagne	Champagne	sparkling
	Chardonnay	California	dry white
	Gewürztraminer VT	Alsace	demi-sec white
	Orvieto Abbocado	Italy	demi-sec white
	Sémillon	New World	dry white
	Viognier	New World	dry white
JAMBALAYA	Poulsard	Jura	dry white
	Sancerre	Loire	dry white
	Sauvignon Blanc	New Zealand	dry white

FOOD	WINE NAME	REGION/ COUNTRY	WINE STYLE
JAPANESE	Champagne NV	Champagne	sparkling
FOOD	Pomerol	Bordeaux	dry red
	Pouilly-Fuissé	Burgundy	dry white
	Riesling	Germany	dry white
	Seyval Blanc	England	dry white
KANGAROO	Cabernet Sauvignon	Australia	dry red
	Chardonnay	Australia	dry white
	Shiraz	Australia	dry red
KEDGEREE	Champagne	Champagne	sparkling
	Chardonnay	New World	dry white
	Pinot Blanc	Alsace	dry white
KIPPERS	Champagne	Champagne	sparkling
	Corbières	Languedoc	dry white
	Entre-Deux-Mers	Bordeaux	dry white
KIDNEYS	Beaujolais	Beaujolais	dry red
	Cabernet Sauvignon	New World	dry red
	Pommard	Burgundy	dry red
KLEFTIKO	Nemea	Greece	dry red
	Periquita	Portugal	dry red
	Poulsard	Arbois	dry red
KOUGELHOPF	Quarts de Chaume	Loire	sweet white
	Riesling SGN	Alsace	sweet white
	Pinot Gris VT	Alsace	sweet white
LAMB	Cabernet Sauvignon	Australia	dry red
	Pauillac or Médoc	Bordeaux	dry red
	Rioja or Navarra	Spain	dry red
LAMB, crown roast	Ajaccio	Corsica	dry red
	St-Julien	Bordeaux	dry red
LAMB, CURRIED	Gewürztraminer	Alsace	dry white
	Pinot Noir	California	dry red
	Savigny-Les-Beaune	Burgundy	dry red
	Shiraz	Australia	dry red

FOOD	WINE NAME	REGION/ COUNTRY	WINE STYLE
LAMB, with HERBES DE PROVENCE			
	Cinsault or Mourvèdre	New World	dry red
	Colli Orientali del Friuli	Italy	dry red
	Côtes de Provence	Provence	dry rose
	Dão	Portugal	dry red
	Pinot Nero Alto Adige	Italy	dry red
	St-Emilion	Bordeaux	dry red
LAMB, shoulder	Côtes de Bourg	Bordeaux	dry red
	Hermitage	Rhône	dry red
	Moulin-à-Vent	Beaujolais	dry red
LAMB KEBABS	Arbois	Jura	dry red
	Côtes de Provence	Provence	dry rosé
	Patrimonio	Corsica	dry red
	St-Joseph	Rhône	dry red
LAMB, roast, with MINT sauce	Champagne rosé	Champagne	sparkling
	Margaux	Bordeaux	dry red
	Mavrud	Bulgaria	dry red
	Pommard	Burgundy	dry red
	Vino Nobile di Montepulciano	Italy	dry red
LAMB CHOPS, grilled	Côtes de Provence	Provence	dry rosé
	Lirac	Rhône	dry rosé
	Pomerol	Bordeaux	dry red
	Saumur Champigny	Loire	dry red
LAMB STEW (see STEWS and CASSEROLES)			
LASAGNE	Barbera d'Asti	Italy	dry red
	Chianti	Italy	dry red
	St-Amour	Beaujolais	dry red
LINGUINE with CLAM SAUCE (see PASTAS with CLAM SAUCE)			
LINGUINE with PESTO SAUCE (see PASTAS with PESTO SAUCE)			
LIVER	Champagne	Champagne	sparkling
	Côtes de Provence	Provence	dry rosé
	Médoc	Bordeaux	dry red
	Rioja	Spain	dry red

FOOD	WINE NAME	REGION/ COUNTRY	WINE STYLE
LOBSTER	Bordeaux sec	Bordeaux	dry white
	Champagne		
	(Blancs de Blancs)	Champagne	sparkling
	Chardonnay	California	dry white
	Condrieu	Rhône	dry white
	Meursault	Burgundy	dry white
LOBSTER BISQUE (see CLAM CHOWDER)			
LOTTE (see also FISH or SEAFOOD)			
	Champagne		
	(Blanc de Blancs)	Champagne	sparkling
	Muscadet	Loire	dry white
	Mâcon	Burgundy	dry white
MACARONI AND CHEESE			
	Beaujolais	Burgundy	dry red
	Soave	Italy	dry white
MACKEREL with BUTTER and SPRING ONIONS			
	Chablis (oaked)	Burgundy	dry white
	Gaillac	Rhône	dry white
	Graves	Bordeaux	dry whte
	Sémillon	New World	dry white
MACKEREL with GREEN GOOSEBERRY SAUCE			
	Gros Plant	Loire/Nantes	dry white
	Muscadet	Loire	dry white
	Sancerre	Loire/Centre	dry red
	Vinho Verde	Portugal	dry white
MEAT	Bordeaux Supérieur	Bordeaux	dry red
LOAF	Cabernet Sauvignon	California	dry red
	Pinot Noir	New World	dry red
	Zinfandel	California	dry red
MELANZANE	Barbaresco	Italy	dry red
ALLA	Barolo	Italy	dry red
PARMIGIANA	Brunello di Montalcino	Italy	dry red
	Rosato di Salento	Italy	dry rosé
MELON	Pineau de Charentes	Cognac	vin de liqueur
with PORT	Monbazillac	Bordeaux	sweet white

FOOD	WINE NAME	REGION/ COUNTRY	WINE STYLE
MELON	Bardolino	Italy	dry red
with	Bergerac	Southwest France	dry red
PARMA	Bianco di Scandiano	Italy	dry white
HAM	Chinon	Loire	dry red
	St-Joseph	Rhône	dry red
MERGUEZ	Grenache	New World	dry red
SAUSAGES	Rioja	Spain	dry red
	Shiraz	Australia	dry red
MERINGUES	Asti Spumante	Italy	sparkling
	Champagne	Champagne	sparkling
	Muscat de Rivesaltes	Roussillon	*vin doux naturel*
MEXICAN	Côtes du Rhône	Rhône	dry red
FOOD	Fitou	Languedoc	dry red
	Valpolicella	Italy	dry red
MILLE	Champagne	Champagne	sparkling
FEUILLES	Pacherenc du Vic-Bilh	Southwest France	sweet white
MINCE PIES	Pacherenc du Vic-Bilh	Southwest France	sweet white
	Port	Portugal	fortified red
	Vouvray	Loire	sweet white
MINESTRONE	Alenquir	Portugal	dry white
	Chianti	Italy	dry white
	Corbières	Languedoc	dry white
MONKFISH (see also FISH or SEAFOOD)			
	Chardonnay	Chile	dry white
	Puligny-Montrachet	Burgundy	dry white
	Sémillon	Australia	dry white
MOULES	Muscadet	Loire	dry white
ET FRITES	Sancerre	Loire/Centre	dry white
	Verdicchio	Italy	dry white
MOULES	Chablis	Burgundy	dry white
MARINIERS	Entre-Deux-Mers	Bordeaux	dry white
	Pouilly-Fumé	Loire	dry white
	Riesling	Alsace	dry white

FOOD	WINE NAME	REGION/ COUNTRY	WINE STYLE
MOUSSAKA	Côtes du Rhône	Rhône	dry red
	Dão	Portugal	dry red
	Kékfrankos	Hungary	dry red
	Naoussa	Greece	dry red
	Nemea	Greece	dry red
	Pinotage	South Africa	dry red
	Rioja	Spain	dry red

MUSHROOMS (see MUSHROOMS AND WINE on page 86)

MUSSELS (see MOULES)

NUTS (almonds, walnuts, hazelnuts, peanuts)

	WINE NAME	REGION/ COUNTRY	WINE STYLE
	Amontillado	Spain	fortified red
	Madeira	Spain	fortified red
	Manzanilla	Spain	fortified white
	Port	Portugal	fortified white
OCTOPUS	Bellet	Provence	dry white
	Gigondas rosé	Rhône	dry rosé
	Rioja	Spain	dry white
	Zinfandel	California	dry white
OLIVES	Amontillado	Spain	fortified red
	Côtes de Provence	Provence	dry white
	Manzanilla	Spain	fortified white
	Riesling	Alsace	dry white
	Sherry	Spain	fortified red
OMELETTE	Brouilly	Beaujolais	dry red
	Champagne	Champagne	sparkling
	Pinot Blanc	Alsace	dry white
	Sancerre	Loire/Centre	dry white

OMELETTE with BACON

| | Pinot Gris | Alsace | dry white |

OMELETTE with CHEESE

| | Chardonnay | New World | dry white |
| | Pinot Blanc | Alsace | dry white |

OMELETTE with TOMATO

| | Beaujolais | Burgundy | dry red |
| | Chianti | Italy | dry red |

FOOD	WINE NAME	REGION/ COUNTRY	WINE STYLE
OMELETTE with MUSHROOMS			
	Côtes du Rhône	Rhône	dry red
OMELETTE with TRUFFLES			
	Meursault	Burgundy	dry white
	Champagne	Champagne	sparkling white
ONIONS,	Gewürztraminer	Alsace	dry white
CREAMED	Palette	Provence	dry white
	Riesling	Alsace	dry white
ONION	Arbois rosé	Jura	dry rosé
TART	Corbières	Languedoc	dry white
	Pinot Blanc	Alsace	dry white
	Pinot Gris	Alsace	dry white
ORANGE (see DESSERTS with a base of FRUIT)			
OSSO BUCCO	Barbera	Italy	dry red
	Crozes-Hermitage	Rhône	dry white
	Dolcetto d'Alba	Italy	dry red
	Gigondas	Rhône	dry red
	Patrimonio	Corsica	dry red
	Valpolicella	Italy	dry red
OXTAIL	Brunello di Montalcino	Italy	dry red
	Châteauneuf-du-Pape	Rhône	dry red
	Periquita	Portugal	dry red
OYSTERS	Aligoté	Burgundy	dry white
	Entre-Deux-Mers	Bordeaux	dry white
	Gavi	Italy	dry white
	Muscadet	Loire	dry white
	Sancerre	Loire/Centre	dry white
PAELLA	Côtes de Provence	Provence	dry rosé
	Pouilly-Fumé	Loire	dry white
	Rioja	Spain	dry rosé
PARTRIDGE	Châteauneuf-du-Pape	Rhône	dry red
	Pomerol	Bordeaux	dry red

FOOD	WINE NAME	REGION/ COUNTRY	WINE STYLE
PASTAS with CARBONARA SAUCE			
	Barbera	Italy	dry white
	Bardolino	Italy	dry red
	Chardonnay Alto Adige	Italy	dry white
	Mâcon	Burgundy	dry white
	Marino Superiore	Italy	dry white
PASTAS with CLAM SAUCE			
	Chardonnay (unoaked)	New World	dry white
	Chasselas	Alsace	dry white
	Corvo Bianco	Italy	dry white
	Pinot Grigio	Italy	dry white
PASTAS with CREAM SAUCE			
	Barbera d'Asti	Italy	dry red
	Bardolino	Italy	dry red
	Montepulciano d'Abruzzo	Italy	dry red
	Rosso Piceno Superiore	Italy	dry red
	Sangiovese	California	dry red
PASTAS with PESTO SAUCE			
	Barbera d'Asti	Italy	dry red
	Chardonnay (unoaked)	New World	dry white
	Lugana	Italy	dry white
	St-Emilion	Bordeaux	dry red
	Soave	Italy	dry white
PASTAS, SPINACH and RICOTTA			
	Bianco di Custoza	Italy	dry white
	Chianti	Italy	dry white
	Grave del Friuli	Italy	sparkling
PASTA PRIMAVERA	Colli Berici		
	Pinot Bianco	Italy	dry white
	Pinot Grigio	Italy	dry white
	Sauvignon Blanc	New Zealand	dry white
PATE (see FOIE GRAS)			
PEA and HAM SOUP			
	Chardonnay	Chile	dry white
	Pinotage	South Africa	dry red

FOOD	WINE NAME	REGION/ COUNTRY	WINE STYLE
PECAN PIE	Champagne	Champagne	sparkling
	Ice wine	Canada	sweet white
	Sauternes	Bordeaux	sweet white
PEPPERS,	Bandol rosé	Provence	dry rosé
roasted	Bellet rosé	Provence	dry rosé
or stuffed	Mâcon	Burgundy	dry white
	Regaleali Rosato	Italy	dry rosé
	Pinot Gris	Alsace	dry white
PESTO SAUCE (see PASTAS with PESTO SAUCE)			
PHEASANT	Barolo	Italy	dry red
	Chambolle-Musigny	Burgundy	dry red
	Crozes-Hermitage	Rhône	dry red
	Pomerol	Bordeaux	dry red
	St-Emilion	Bordeaux	dry red
PIGEON	Buzet	Southwest France	dry red
	Crozes-Hermitage	Rhône	dry red
	Pinotage	South Africa	dry red
	St-Emilion	Bordeaux	dry red
	Vacqueyras	Rhône	dry red
PISSALADIERE	Bellet rosé	Provence	dry rosé
	Tavel	Rhône	dry rosé
PIKE WITH GARLIC (see also FISH or SEAFOOD)			
	Riesling	Austria	dry white
	Sauvignon Blanc	Australia	dry white
	Sylvaner	Alsace	dry white
PIPPERADA	Bandol rosé	Provence	dry rosé
	Chacoli	Southwest France	dry white
	Champagne rosé	Champagne	sparkling
	Pacherenc du Vic-Bilh	Southwest France	dry white
PIZZA	Barbera d'Asti	Italy	dry red
	Cabernet Sauv./Cinsault	Lebanon	dry red
	Chianti	Italy	dry red
	Côte de Beaune	Burgundy	dry red
	Sangiovese	California	dry red
	Zinfandel	California	dry red

FOOD	WINE NAME	REGION/ COUNTRY	WINE STYLE
PIZZA,	Bianco di Custoza	Italy	dry white
seafood	Côtes de Provence rosé	Provence	dry rosé
	Pouilly-Fumé	Loire	dry white
	Sauvignon Blanc	New World	dry white
POLENTA	Ajaccio rosé	Corsica	dry rosé
	Côtes de Provence rosé	Provence	dry rosé
	Vin de Corse	Corsica	dry red
PORK, ROAST	Bairrada	Portugal	dry red
	Chardonnay	New World	dry white
	Chianti	Italy	dry red
	Tempranillo	Spain	dry red
	Pinot Gris	Alsace	dry white
PORK, roast, with MUSTARD SAUCE			
	Gewürztraminer VT	Alsace	sweet white
	Riesling Spätlese	Germany	sweet white
PORK CHOPS	Corbières	Languedoc	dry red
	Côtes de Duras	Southwest France	dry red
	Pinot Gris	Alsace	dry white
	Pinot Noir	New World	dry red
POT-AU-FEU	Anjou	Loire	dry red
	Bergerac	Southwest France	dry red
	St-Emilion	Bordeaux	dry red
POT ROAST	Riesling	Alsace	dry white
	Gewürztraminer	Alsace	dry white
	St-Emilion	Bordeaux	dry red
POTATO SALAD	Côtes de Provence	Provence	dry rosé
	Pinot Noir	Alsace	dry red
	Riesling	Alsace	dry white
PRAWNS	Champagne	Champagne	sparkling
	Chassagne-Montrachet	Burgundy	dry white
	Sauvignon Blanc	New Zealand	dry white
	Sauvignon Colli		
	Orientali del Friuli	Italy	dry white
	Soave	Italy	dry white

FOOD	WINE NAME	REGION/ COUNTRY	WINE STYLE
PROSCIUTTO	Barbera	Italy	dry red
	Pinot Grigio	Italy	dry white
	Valpolicella Classico	Italy	dry red
PUMPKIN PIE	Monbazillac	Bordeaux	sweet white
	Savennières	Loire	dry white
	Sémillon	New World	sweet white
QUAIL	Champagne	Champagne	sparkling
	Pinot Noir	Alsace	dry red
	St-Emilion	Bordeaux	dry red
	Saumur-Champigny	Loire	dry red
	Volnay	Burgundy	dry red
QUAIL'S EGGS	Champagne	Champagne	sparkling
QUICHE	Bergerac	Southwest France	dry white
LORRAINE	Bianco di Custoza	Italy	dry white
	Chinon	Loire	dry red
	Pinot Gris	Alsace	dry white
	Riesling	Alsace	dry white
RABBIT	Côtes de Duras	Southwest France	dry red
	Côte de Nuits	Burgundy	dry red
	Pinot Noir	New World	dry red
	St-Estèphe	Bordeaux	dry red
	Volnay	Burgundy	dry red
RACLETTE	Chasselas	Alsace or Switz.	dry white
	Côtes du Rhône	Rhône	dry red
	Pinot Gris	Alsace	dry white
	Varois	Switzerland	dry red
RATATOUILLE	Corbières	Languedoc	dry red
	Côtes de Provence	Provence	dry rosé
	Minervois	Languedoc	dry red
	Zinfandel	California	dry red
RISOTTO	Côtes du Rhône	Rhône	dry red
ALLA	Pinot Grigio	Italy	dry white
MILANESE	Soave	Italy	dry white
	Trebbiano d'Abruzzo	Italy	dry red

FOOD	WINE NAME	REGION/ COUNTRY	WINE STYLE
RISOTTO ALLA PARMIGIANA (see also CHEESE AND WINE on page 87)			
	Bardolino	Italy	dry red
	Bianco di Custoza	Italy	dry white
	Dolcetto d'Alba	Italy	dry red
ROQUEFORT (see CHEESE AND WINE on page 87)			
SACHERTORTE	Riesling TBA	Germany	sweet white
	Beaumes-de-Venise	Roussillon	*vin doux naturel*
	Champagne	Champagne	sparkling
SALAD, CAESAR	Chardonnay	New York	dry white
	Champagne	Champagne	sparkling
	Rully	Burgundy	dry white
SALAD, CHEF'S (eggs, tomatoes, cheese)			
	Chardonnay	Chile	dry white
	Soave	Italy	dry white
	Viognier	California	dry white
SALAD, CHICKEN	Beaujolais	Burgundy	dry red
	Bordeaux rosé	Bordeaux	dry rosé
	Chardonnay	Chile	dry white
	Sauvignon Blanc	New Zealand	dry white
SALAD, GREEN, with OIL and VINEGAR			
	Aligoté	Burgundy	dry white
	Cheverny	Loire	dry white
	Muscadet	Loire	dry white
	Sancerre	Loire/Centre	dry white
	Vinho Verde	Portugal	dry white
SALAD, NICOISE	Cheverny	Loire	dry white
	Coteaux d'Aix-en-Provence rosé	Provence	dry rosé
	Côtes du Rhône	Rhône	dry red
SALAD, SEAFOOD	Soave	Italy	dry white
	Verdicchio	Italy	dry white
SALAD, TOMATOES	Barbera	Italy	dry red
	Riesling Spätlese	Germany	sweet white
	Sauvignon Blanc	New Zealand	dry white

FOOD	WINE NAME	REGION/ COUNTRY	WINE STYLE
SALAD, TUNA	Côtes de Provence rosé	Provence	dry rosé
	Valpolicella	Italy	dry red
	Vin de Corse	Corsica	dry white
SALAD, WALDORF	Beaumes-de-Venise	Roussillon	*vin doux naturel*
	Riesling VT	Alsace	sweet white
	Sauternes	Bordeaux	sweet white
SALAMI	Barbera	Italy	dry red
	Bardolino	Italy	dry red
	Montepulciano d'Abruzzo	Italy	dry red
	Rosso Cònero	Italy	dry red
	Tavel rosé	Rhône	dry rosé
	Zinfandel	California	dry red
SALMON, cold	Chardonnay	New World	dry white
	Coteaux d'Aix-en-Provence	Provence	dry rosé
	Pinot Noir	Alsace	dry red
SALMON, cooked	Chablis	Burgundy	dry white
	Chinon	Loire	dry red
	Condrieu	Rhône	dry white
	Sancerre	Loire/Centre	dry white
SALMON, smoked	Champagne brut	Champagne	sparkling
	Chardonnay	New World	dry white
	Riesling	Alsace	dry white
	Rully	Burgundy	dry white
SALT COD BALLS	Chinon	Loire	dry red
	Rioja	Spain	dry white
	Tempranillo	Spain	dry red
SALTIMBOCCA ALLA ROMANA	Barbera d'Asti	Italy	dry red
	Rosso Cònero	Italy	dry rosé
	Sangiovese	California	dry red
SALSA (red and green)	Sauvignon Blanc	New World	dry white
	Vinho Verde	Portugal	dry white

SANDWICHES (see principal ingredient)

FOOD	WINE NAME	REGION/ COUNTRY	WINE STYLE
SARDINES	Gaillac	Southwest France	dry white
	Orvieto	Italy	dry white
	Vinho Verde	Portugal	dry white
SASHIMI	Riesling Kabinett	Germany	dry white
	Sancerre	Loire/Centre	dry white
	Sauvignon Blanc	New Zealand	dry white
SATAY	Pinot Gris	Alsace	dry white
	Rully	Burgundy	dry white
SAUCE, BEARNAISE	Frascati	Italy	demi-sec white
	Riesling Kabinett	Germany	dry white
	Sancerre	Loire/Centre	dry white
	Vouvray	Loire	demi-sec white
SAUCE, BOLOGNAISE (BOLOGNESE)			
	Cabernet Sauvignon	Australia	dry red
	Merlot	Chile	dry red
	Montepulciano d'Abruzzo	Italy	dry red
	Rosso Cònero	Italy	dry red
SAUCE, CHASSEUR (see CHICKEN, SAUCE CHASSEUR)			
SAUCE, CHILE	Côtes du Rhône	Rhône	dry red
	Fitou	Languedoc	dry red
	Shiraz	Australia	dry red
SAUCE, CRANBERRY	Mourvèdre	France or NW	dry red
	Riesling Kabinett	Germany	dry white
	Shiraz	Australia	dry red
SAUCE, HOLLANDAISE	Bâtard-Montrachet	Burgundy	dry white
	Sancerre	Loire/Centre	dry white
	Vouvray	Loire	dry white
SAUCE, HORSERADISH	Riesling	Alsace	dry white
	Sancerre	Loire/Centre	dry white
	Shiraz	Australia	dry red
SAUCE, MAYONNAISE	Chablis (unoaked)	Burgundy	dry white
	Chardonnay (unoaked)	New World	dry white

FOOD	WINE NAME	REGION/ COUNTRY	WINE STYLE
SAUCE,	Cabernet Sauvignon	Australian	dry red
MINT	Gevrey-Chambertin	Burgundy	dry red
	Pomerol	Bordeaux	dry red
SAUCE,	Chardonnay	Chile	dry white
MUSTARD	Riesling	Alsace	dry white
	Sancerre	Loire/Centre	dry white
SAUCE,	Mourvèdre	France or NW	dry red
PEPPER	Pomerol	Bordeaux	dry red
	Pommard	Burgundy	dry red
	Shiraz	Australia	dry red
	Zinfandel	Califonia	dry red

SAUCE, RED WINE
Use the same wine that is used in the sauce

	Barbaresco	Italy	dry red
	Brunello di Montalcino	Italy	dry red
	Cabernet Sauvignon	New World	dry red
	Côtes du Rhône	Rhône	dry red
SAUCE,	Gewürztraminer	Alsace	dry white
SWEET-	Pinot Gris VT	Alsace	semi-dry white
and-SOUR	Vouvray	Alsace	sweet white
SAUCE,	Aligoté	Burgundy	dry white
TOMATO	Sancerre	Loire/Centre	dry white
	Sauvignon Blanc	New World	dry white
SAUCE,	Cheverny	Loire	dry white
VINAIGRETTE	Pouilly-Fumé	Loire	dry white
	Vinho Verde	Portugal	dry white
SAUCE,	Chardonnay	New World	dry white
WHITE	Chassagne-Montrachet	Burgundy	dry white
	Meursault	Burgundy	dry white
SAUCE,	Chablis	Burgundy	dry white
WHITE	Graves	Bordeaux	dry white
WINE	Muscadet	Loire	dry white
	Pinot Gris VT	Alsace	semisweet white
	Sauvignon Blanc	New World	dry white

FOOD	WINE NAME	REGION/ COUNTRY	WINE STYLE
SAUERBRATEN	Baden Spätburgunder	Germany	dry red
	Barbaresco	Italy	dry red
	Gewürztraminer VT	Alsace	demi-sec white
	Morgon	Beaujolais	dry red
	Pinot Noir	Alsace	dry red
SCALLOPS, in CREAM and TARRAGON			
	Bâtard-Montrachet	Burgundy	dry white
	Champagne	Champagne	sparkling
	Meursault	Burgundy	dry white
	Sauvignon Blanc	New Zealand	dry white
SCALLOPS,	Graves	Bordeaux	dry white
grilled	Muscadet	Loire	dry white
	Savennières	Loire	dry white
SEAFOOD (see also FISH)			
	Bianco di Custoza	Italy	dry white
	Sancerre	Loire/Centre	dry white
	Sauvignon Blanc	New World	dry white
	Verdicchio	Italy	dry white
SHELLFISH (see SEAFOOD)			
SHEPHERD'S	Bourgueil	Loire	dry red
PIE	Buzet	Southwest France	dry red
	Pomerol	Bordeaux	dry red
SHRIMP	Bergerac	Southwest France	dry white
COCKTAIL	Muscadet	Loire	dry white
	Sauvignon Blanc	New World	dry white
SNAILS (see ESCARGOTS à la BOURGUIGNONNE)			
SOLE	Bellet	Provence	dry white
MEUNIERE	Chablis	Burgundy	dry white
	Condrieu	Rhône	dry white
	Riesling	Alsace	dry white
SORBETS (see also DESSERTS)			
	Champagne	Champagne	sparkling
	Pineau de Charentes	Cognac	vin de liqueur

FOOD	WINE NAME	REGION/ COUNTRY	WINE STYLE
SOUFFLE, BROCCOLI and CHEESE			
	Champagne	Champagne	sparkling
	Muscadet sur lie	Loire	dry white
	Rully	Burgundy	dry white
	Sauvignon Blanc	New Zealand	dry white
SOUFFLE, SEAFOOD (see SEAFOOD)			
SOUFFLE, SPINACH	Chardonnay	New World	dry white
	Frascati	Italy	dry white
	St-Véran or Mâcon	Burgundy	dry white
	Vin du Jura	Jura	dry white
SPICES and HERBS (see PART 2)			
SQUID, cooked in own juices			
	Ajaccio	Corsica	dry red
	Côtes de Bordeaux	Bordeaux	dry white
	Gaillac	France	dry white
	Mâcon	Burgundy	dry white
	Valdepeñas	Spain	dry red
STEAK, SIRLOIN	Barolo	Italy	dry red
	Cabernet Sauvignon	California	dry red
	Chianti Classico	Italy	dry red
	Merlot	New World	dry red
	Pomerol	Bordeaux	dry red
	Shiraz	Australia	dry red
STEAK and KIDNEY PIE	Buzet	Southwest France	dry red
	Cahors	Southwest France	dry red
STEAK TARTARE	Cahors	Southwest France	dry red
	Cornas	Rhône	dry red
	Crozes-Hermitage	Rhône	dry red
	St-Amour	Beaujolais	dry red
	St-Véran	Burgundy	dry white
STEWS and CASSEROLES	Amarone	Italy	dry red
	Brunello di Montalcino	Italy	dry red
	Cahors	Southwest France	dry red
	Copertino	Italy	dry red
	Cornas	Rhône	dry red
	Pauillac	Bordeaux	dry red

FOOD	WINE NAME	REGION/ COUNTRY	WINE STYLE
STEWS and	Periquita	Portugal	dry red
CASSEROLES	Shiraz	Australia	dry red
(continued)	Vino Nobile di		
	Montepulciano	Italy	dry red

STILTON (see CHEESE AND WINE on page 87)

STIR-FRIES	Pinot Grigio	Italy	dry white
	Riesling	Alsace	dry white
	Sauvignon Blanc	New World	dry white
SUSHI	Arbois	Jura	dry white
	Riesling Kabinett	Germany	dry white
	Sancerre	Loire/Centre	dry white
SWEETBREADS	Côte de Beaune	Burgundy	dry red
	Côtes de Provence rosé	Provence	dry rosé
	Sylvaner	Alsace	dry white
SWEET	Monbazillac	Sauternes	sweet white
POTATOES	Crozes-Hermitage	Rhône	dry white

SWORDFISH (see FISH or SEAFOOD)

TABBOULEH	Bandol rosé	Provence	dry rosé
	Bellet rosé	Provence	dry rosé
	Côtes du Jura	Jura	dry red
TAPAS	Amontillado	Spain	fortified red
	Bandol rosé	Provence	dry rosé
	Fino Sherry	Spain	fortified white
	Sancerre	Loire/Centre	dry white
TAPENADE	Lirac	Rhône	dry rosé
	Palette	Provence	dry red
	Patrimonio	Corsica	dry red
TARAMASALATA	Chablis	Burgundy	dry white
	Muscadet	Loire	dry white
	Patrimonio	Corsica	dry white
	Sancerre rosé	Loire/Centre	dry rosé

FOOD	WINE NAME	REGION/ COUNTRY	WINE STYLE
TEMPURA	Sancerre	Loire/Centre	dry white
	Chablis	Burgundy	dry white
	Orvieto	Italy	dry white
THAI FOOD	Chablis	Burgundy	dry white
	Colombard	New World	dry white
	Gewürztraminer	Alsace	dry white
	Sauvignon Blanc	New World	dry white
	Tokàji	Hungary	dry white
	Vin de Paille	Juras	sweet white

TIRAMISU (see also DESSERTS with a base of COFFEE)

	Muscat de Rivesaltes	Roussillon	*vin doux naturel*
	Sauternes	Bordeaux	sweet white

TOMATOES (see SAUCE, TOMATO)

FOOD	WINE NAME	REGION/COUNTRY	WINE STYLE
TONGUE	Bergerac	Southwest France	dry red
	Cahors	Southwest France	dry red
	Chardonnay	Chile	dry white
TRIPE	Mersault	Burgundy	dry white
	Pacherenc du Vic-Bilh	Southwest France	dry white
	Pouilly-Fumé	Loire	dry white

TROUT (see FISH or SEAFOOD)

TRUFFLES, both black and white

	Barbaresco	Italy	dry red
	Cahors	Southwest France	dry red
	Champagne (Blanc de Blancs)	Champagne	sparkling
	Chassagne-Montrachet	Burgundy	dry white
	Echezeaux	Burgundy	dry red
	Pomerol	Bordeaux	dry red
	Vosne-Romanée	Burgundy	dry red

TUNA (see FISH and SALAD, TUNA)

TURBOT (see FISH)

TURKEY, roast, with Thanksgiving trimmings

	Chardonnay	California	dry red
	Châteauneuf-du-Pape	Rhône	dry red
	Vosne-Romanée	Burgundy	dry red
	Zinfandel	California	dry red

FOOD	WINE NAME	REGION/ COUNTRY	WINE STYLE
VANILLA (see DESSERTS with a base of VANILLA)			
VEAL	Côte de Beaune	Burgundy	dry red
	Graves	Bordeaux	dry white
	Margaux	Bordeaux	dry red
	Pinot Gris	Alsace	dry white
VEGETABLES (grilled or roasted)			
	Beaujolais Villages	Burgundy	dry red
	Cassis	Provence	dry white
	Corbières	Languedoc	dry white
	Palette	Provence	dry white
	Rueda	Spain	dry white
	St-Joseph	Rhône	dry white
VEGETABLES (raw)	Bardolino	Italy	dry red
	Beaujolais	Burgundy	dry red
	Sauvignon Blanc	New World	dry white
VENISON with CRANBERRIES or JUNIPER BERRIES			
	Bandol	Provence	dry red
	Chambertin	Burgundy	dry red
	Cinsault/ Cabernet Sauvignon	Lebanon	dry red
	Mourvèdre	New World	dry red
	Shiraz	Australia	dry red
	Zinfandel	California	dry red
VICHYSSOISE	Bergerac	Southwest France	dry white
	Sancerre	Loire/Centre	dry white
	Vacqueyras	Rhône	dry white
WILD BOAR	Bandol	Provence	dry red
	Cinsault/Cab. Sauv.	Lebanon	dry red
	Gigondas	Rhône	dry red
	Pomerol	Bordeaux	dry red
	Pommard	Burgundy	dry red
	Shiraz	Australia	dry red
	Vino Nobile de Montepulciano	Italy	dry red
WEINER SCHNITZEL	Grüner Veltliner	Austria	dry white
	Weissburgunder	Germany	dry red
	Sancerre	Loire/Centre	dry white
	Chinon	Loire	dry red

WINE TO FOOD INDEX

WINE	REGION	WINE TYPE	FOOD
Ajaccio	Corsica	Red	Lamb crown roast, Roast pork, Spicy sausages, Squid cooked in their own juices
		Rosé	Polenta, Bouillabaisse, Ratatouille
Alenquir	Portugal	Dry white	Grilled sardines, Minestrone, Salt cod balls, Tapas
Aligoté	Burgundy	Dry white	Cod, Blue cheese dip, Escargots à la Bourguignonne, Oysters and mussels, Green salad with oil and vinegar dressing, Tomato sauce dishes, Trout
Alto Adige Chardonnay	Italy	Dry white	Chicken salad, Fettuccine Alfredo, Pasta with carbonara sauce, Savory crêpes, Tuna salad
Amarone della Valpolicella	Italy	Dry red	Risotto alla Parmigiana, Red meat stews and casseroles
Amontillado Sherry	Spain	Fortified red	Almonds, walnuts, hazelnuts, and peanuts, Chorizo, Manchego and ewe's milk cheeses, Olives and tapas, Wild boar
Anjou	Loire	Dry red	Bacon and ham dishes, Charcuterie, Pot-au-feu, White meats. See also Bourgueil and Chinon
Arbois	Jura	Red	Game, Spicy meat dishes, Sushi
		Rosé	Chutney, Lamb dishes, Onion tart
		White	Andouillette grilled with mustard, Brussels sprouts, Cauliflower cheese, Chicken curry, Cognac-based desserts, Haddock and white fish dishes, Kebabs

WINE	REGION	WINE TYPE	FOOD
Asti Spumante	Italy	Sparkling	Chestnut-, mint-, or fruit-based desserts, Christmas pudding, Meringues
Baden Spätburgunder	Germany	Dry red	Goulash, Beef stews and casseroles, Sauerbraten
Bairrada	Portugal	Dry red	Garlic-based sauces, Roast pork, Roast vegetables in oil and herbs
Bandol	Provence	Red	Barbecued meats, Boeuf en daube, Ravioli niçoise, Roast vegetables, Venison with cranberries or juniper berry sauce. *See also* Palette
		Rosé	Wild boar, Anchovies or anchovy paste, Fish and chips, Roasted or stuffed peppers, Pipperada, Salade niçoise, Tabbouleh, Tapas
Banyuls	Roussillon	*Vin doux naturel*	Chocolate-, coffee-, or strawberry-based desserts, Christmas pudding
Barbaresco	Italy	Dry red	Eggplant with Parmesan, Cassoulet, Fish in red wine and red wine sauce dishes, Sauerbraten, Truffles, black and white. *See also* Barolo
Barbera d'Asti	Italy	Dry red	Anchovy paste and dips, Bolognese sauce, Lasagne and pizza or pasta with meat and cream sauce, Osso bucco, Pasta with carbonara or pesto sauce, Prosciutto, Risottos, especially mushroom, Salami-based dishes, Saltimbocca alla Romana, Tomato salad. *See also* Dolcetto d'Alba
Bardolino	Italy	Dry red	Antipasti and charcuterie, Melon with Parma ham, Pasta with carbonara sauce, Pasta dishes with meat and béchamel sauce, Raw vegetables, Risotto alla Parmigiana and other risottos, Salami-based dishes

WINE	REGION	WINE TYPE	FOOD
Barolo	Italy	Dry red	Eggplant with Parmesan, Beef bourguignonne, Boeuf en daube, Brasato al Barolo, Game, grouse, and pheasant, Sirloin steak. See also Barbaresco
Barsac	Bordeaux	Sweet white	Caramel- and fruit-based desserts, Pâtés and terrines, Spicy ethnic foods. See also Cadillac, Loupiac, Monbazillac, Ste-Croix-du-Mont, Sauternes
Bâtard-Montrachet	Burgundy	Dry white	Hollandaise sauce, Most butter- or cream-based sauces, Scallops in cream and tarragon sauce, White fish dishes. See also Meursault
Beaujolais	Burgundy	Dry red	Bacon and ham, Charcuterie and boudin blanc (white pudding), Chicken salad, Grilled, roast, and raw vegetables, Hamburgers, Kidneys, Macaroni and cheese, Mexican and chile dishes, Raspberry-based desserts
Bellet	Provence	Rosé	Pissaladière (onion, olive, and anchovy tart), Roast or stuffed peppers, Tabbouleh
		White	Octopus, Salade niçoise, Sole meunière
Bergerac	Southwest France	Red	Bean and pasta soup, Fried fish, Potted or jugged hare, Melon with Parma ham, Pot-au-feu, Roast meats, both white and red, Tongue
		White	Cassis-based desserts, Fish and chips, Quiche lorraine, Prawn cocktail, Vichyssoise
Bianco di Custoza	Italy	Dry white	Pasta with spinach and ricotta, Pizza with seafood and other seafood dishes, Quiche lorraine, Risotto alla Parmigiana
Bianco di Scandiano	Italy	Dry white	Melon with Parma ham, Pasta with cream and cheese sauces, Poached oysters in vegetable broth, Seafood dishes

WINE	REGION	WINE TYPE	FOOD
Black Muscat	California	Sweet white	Cherry-based desserts, Chocolate, Caramelized oranges
Blanquette de Limoux	Languedoc	Sparkling	Apricot- and cherry-based desserts, Lemon chicken, Sweet and savory soufflés
Bonnes-Mares	Burgundy	Dry red	Beef and chicken potpies, Dry sausages, Hare, game, grouse, and partridge, Mushroom and red wine sauces, Roast duck or goose, Savory cheese dishes. See also Pinot Noir
Bordeaux and Bordeaux Supérieur		Red	Barbecued red meats, Cold lamb or beef, Croque monsieur or madame, Meat fondue, Southern fried chicken
		Rosé	Aioli, Beef strognanoff, Chicken salad, Indian food with spicy yogurt sauces
		White	Barbecued fish, Haggis, Light white meat dishes, Lobster, Meat loaf, Roast chicken, Savory crêpes
Bourgueil	Loire	Dry red	Asparagus, Baked beans, Baked ham with pineapple, Chicken chasseur, Smoked eels, Escargots à la Bourguignonne, Shepherd's pie, Stuffed cabbage. See also Chinon and Anjon
Brouilly	Burgundy	Dry red	Beef bourguignonne, Cold meats, Grilled and roast vegetables, Omelette with tomato, Quiches, pizzas
Brunello di Montalcino	Italy	Dry red	Eggplant with Parmesan, Oxtail, Red meat stews and casseroles, Red wine sauce dishes
Buzet	Southwest France	Dry red	Bean and pasta soup, Buffalo wings, Gazpacho, Pigeon, Potted or jugged hare, Shepherd's pie, Southern fried chicken, Steak and kidney pie

WINE	REGION	WINE TYPE	FOOD
Cabernet Sauvignon			All beef dishes. Red wine sauce dishes. Herbs: thyme, rosemary, and mint
	Argentina		Chili con carne, Spiced pork and sausages
	Australia		Bolognese sauce, Kangaroo, Roast lamb with mint sauce
	California		Hamburgers, Meat loaf, Sirloin steak
	Chile		Charcuterie
Cabernet Sauvignon/Cinsault	Lebanon	Dry red	Barbecued meats, Couscous, Lamb with herbes de provence, Pizza bolognese, Venison with cranberry or juniper berry sauce, Wild boar
Cadillac	Bordeaux	Sweet white	Blue cheese dip, Cheesecake, Pineapple-based desserts, Trifle. *See also* Barsac, Loupiac, Monbazillac, Ste-Croix-du-Mont, Sauternes
Cahors	Southwest France	Dry red	Cassoulet, Confit du canard, Duck à l'orange, Mexican dishes, Red meat stews and casseroles, Steak and kidney pie, Steak tartare, Tarragon chicken, Tongue, Truffles, black and white
Cassis	Provence	Dry white	Grilled and roast vegetables, Light lamb dishes
Cava	Spain	Sparkling	Custard desserts, Quiches, Scrambled eggs with smoked salmon, Tapas
Chablis	Burgundy	Dry white	Avocado, Bagels with salmon and cream cheese, Crab, Escargots à la Bourguignonne, Moules marinières, Gougère, Jambon persillé, Salmon, Sole meunière and other white fish dishes, Taramasalata, Tempura, Thai food, White wine sauce dishes. *See also* Chardonnay

WINE	REGION	WINE TYPE	FOOD
Chablis *(continued)*			
		Grand Cru	Almonds, Carrot soup, Clam chowder
		Premier Cru	Chicken in cream and morel sauce
		Oaked	Smoked salmon
		Unoaked	Mayonnaise, Choucroute garni
Chacoli de Guetaria	Spain	Dry white	Chorizo and other dried spicy sausages, Pipperada, Spicy casseroles
Chambertin	Burgundy	Dry red	Grouse and guinea fowl, Venison with cranberry or juniper berry sauce
Chambolle-Musigny	Burgundy	Dry red	Meat and mushroom dishes, Pheasant, Omelette with truffles
Champagne	Champagne	Sparkling	Everything!—also, Acras, Bagels with salmon and cream cheese, Blinis and buttermilk pancakes, Caesar salad, Cheesecake, Cheeses, especially blue and goat's, Chocolate-, coffee-, cognac-, and fruit-based desserts, Christmas pudding, Guacamole, Ice cream and sorbets, Indian food, Japanese food, Kedgeree, Kippers, Lobster, prawns, and scallops in cream and tarragon, Omelettes, Eggs Benedict, Quail, Red cabbage with apples, Soufflés with broccoli, cheese, spinach, or chocolate, Truffles, black and white
		Blanc de Blancs	Escargots, Foie gras, Liver dishes
		Brut	Avocado, Beef Wellington, Smoked salmon
		Demi-sec	Caramel-based desserts, Sweet crêpes
		Nonvintage	Caviar, Chinese food, Indian food

WINE	REGION	WINE TYPE	FOOD
Champagne *(continued)*			
		Rosé	Carpaccio, Cassis-based desserts, Lamb with mint sauce, Lemon chicken, Scrambled eggs with smoked salmon
Chardonnay		Dry white	
Oaked			Kippers, Roast chicken, Smoked salmon, White fish dishes
Burgundy			Artichokes, Asparagus, Bacon, Carrot soup and pea and ham soup, Chef's salad and chicken salad, Cheese fondue, Chicken in cream and morel sauce, Cold salmon and smoked salmon, Croque monsieur or madame, Omelette with cheese and Eggs Benedict, Pasta with clam sauce, Roast pork, Tongue, Soufflé with spinach, White sauce dishes
New World			Blackened fish, Bruschetta, Caesar salad, Clam chowder, Corn bread, Corn chowder and corn on the cob, Fishcakes and grilled bass, Guacamole, Indian food, Kangaroo, Lobster dishes, Mayonnaise, Mustard sauce, Pesto sauce, Scrambled eggs with smoked salmon
Chassagne-Montrachet	Burgundy	Dry white	Mushrooms, Prawns and delicate seafood dishes, Tarragon, Truffles, black and white, White sauces
Chasselas	Alsace or Switzerland	Dry white	Cheese fondue, Chinese food, Crab, Mild curry dishes, Pasta with clam sauce, Raclette
Châteauneuf-du-Pape	Rhône	Dry red	Basque chicken and coq au vin, Caviar, Goose stuffed with prunes, Gratin dauphinois, Oxtail, Partridge, Roast duck, Roast turkey with traditional trimmings

WINE	REGION	WINE TYPE	FOOD
Chénas, see Beaujolais			
Chenin Blanc	Loire or New World	Dry white	Chestnut-based desserts, Grilled fish, Indian food, Lemon chicken and other poultry dishes, Oriental dishes containing soy sauce, garlic, ginger, and honey, Vegetable and fruit salads. See also Vouvray
Cheverny	Loire	Dry white	Green salad with oil and vinegar dressing, Salade niçoise, Vinaigrette sauce
Chianti	Italy	Dry red, Red	Borscht, Brasciola and carpaccio, Goose stuffed with prunes or other fruit, Hamburgers, Lasagne, Omelette with tomato, Pizza bolognese, Roast pork, Sirloin steak
		White	Chicken dishes, Light pasta dishes, Minestrone, Pasta with spinach and ricotta
Chinon	Loire	Dry red	Asparagus, Baked ham and charcuterie, Melon with Parma ham, Poached, steamed, or lightly grilled salmon, Quiche lorraine, Salt cod balls, Sirloin steak with wild mushrooms, Wiener Schnitzel. See also Bourgueil and Anjon
Chiroubles, see Beaujolais			
Clos de Vougeot	Burgundy	Dry red	Beef bourguignonne, Châteaubriand, Game
Colli Berici Pinot Bianco	Italy	Dry white	Pasta with spring vegetables, Seafood dishes
Colli Orientali del Friuli	Italy	Dry red	Lamb with herbes de provence, Lemon chicken, Light pasta dishes
Colombard	New World	Dry white	Melon with Parma ham, Poached white fish dishes, Most salads, Thai food

WINE	REGION	WINE TYPE	FOOD
Condrieu	Rhône	Dry white	Ceviche, Curry, Indian food, Lobster, Poached, steamed, or lightly grilled salmon, Sole meunière. See also Viognier
Copertino	Italy	Dry red	Borscht, Heavy pasta dishes, Red meat stews and casseroles, Spicy and dried sausages
Corbières	Languedoc	Dry red	Cassoulet, Chicken in cream and morel sauce, Basque chicken and coq au vin, Chorizo, Eggplant, Hare, Herring, Kippers, Minestrone, Onion tart, Pork chops, Ratatouille, Roast meats, especially beef, Sausage
Cornas	Rhône	Dry red	Hare, Red meat stews and casseroles, Steak tartare. See also Syrah, Côte Rôtie, Crozes-Hermitage, St-Joseph
Corton	Burgundy	Dry red	Duck, Game, Red meat dishes, Red wine sauce dishes
Corton-Charlemagne	Burgundy	Dry red	Foie gras, Scallops, Veal dishes, White oily fish dishes, White wine sauces with morels
Côte de Beaune	Burgundy	Dry red	Meat fondue, Sweetbreads, Pizza bolognese, Veal dishes
Côte de Brouilly, see Beaujolais			
Côte Rôtie	Rhône	Dry red	Bean and pasta soup, Roast meats, game, and poultry, Smoked meats
Coteaux d'Aix-en-Provence	Provence	Dry rosé or white	Cold salmon, Lamb chops, Salade niçoise
Coteaux du Layon	Loire	Sweet white	Boudin blanc (white pudding), Cheesecake, Fruit-based desserts and fruit salad
Côtes de Bourg	Bordeaux	Dry red	Casseroles and stews, Heavy bean and rice dishes, Lamb shoulder, Pasta in tomato and meat sauces

WINE	REGION	WINE TYPE	FOOD
Côtes de Duras	Southwest France	Dry red	Casseroles and stews, Rabbit and hare, Roast pork dishes
Côtes du Jura	Jura	Red	Corn bread and cornmeal-based dishes, Roast meats, especially lamb and game, Tabbouleh
		White	Soufflé with spinach. See also Arbois, Poulsard
Côtes de Provence	Provence	Red	Anchovy and olive pastes, Brussels sprouts and baked or roast vegetable dishes, Duck à l'orange, Mediterranean dishes
		Rosé	Blanquette de veau, Kebabs, Lamb chops and lamb with herbes de provence, Liver and sweetbreads, Paella, Polenta, Potato and tuna salad, Ratatouille, Salt cod with garlic, oil, and cream, Seafood pizza
		White	Black pudding, Olives
Côtes du Rhône	Rhône	Dry red	Black pudding, Charcuterie, Cheese fondue and raclette, Chicken curry and coq au vin, Chili con carne, Meat fondue, Gougère, Mexican food, Moussaka, Omelette with mushrooms, Red wine sauce dishes, Risotto alla Milanese, Salade niçoise
Côtes du Roussillon	Roussillon	Dry red	Buffalo wings, Escargots à la Bourguignonne
Crémant de Bourgogne	Burgundy	Sparkling	Banana-based desserts, Blinis, Carrot cake
Crémant de Loire	Loire	Sparkling	Creamy fish dishes, Custard-based dishes
Crepy	Savoie	Dry white	Cheese fondue and raclette, Chinese food, Crab, Mild curry dishes, Pasta with clam sauce

WINE	REGION	WINE TYPE	FOOD
Crozes-Hermitage	Rhône	Red	Pigeon and pheasant, Steak tartare, Stuffed cabbage, Tarragon chicken. *See also* Syrah, Cornas, St-Joseph, Côte Rôtie
		White	Candied sweet potatoes, Choucroute garni, Crab, Curried tomato soup, Osso bucco
Dão	Portugal	Dry red	Lamb with herbes de provence, Moussaka and eggplant dishes, Pork dishes
Dolcetto d'Alba	Italy	Dry red	Antipasti, Black pudding, Fonduta, Osso bucco, Pasta with meat sauces, Risotto alla Parmigiana. *See also* Barbera d'Asti
Echezeaux	Burgundy	Dry red	Venison, game, and roast meats, Mushrooms and mushroom sauces, Rich wine sauces, Truffles, black and white. *See also* Vosne-Romanée
Entre-Deux-Mers	Bordeaux	Dry white	Barbecued and blackened fish, Chicken chasseur, Crab, Herring, Kippers, Moules marinières, Oysters
L'Etoile	Jura	Dry white	Asparagus in cream sauce, Clam chowder, Gratin dauphinois, Iles flottantes
Falerno del Massico	Italy	Dry white	Antipasti, Pasta with Parmesan sauce, Veal dishes
Fino Sherry	Spain	Fortified white	Almonds, Anchovies or anchovy paste, Olives, Tapas
Fitou	Languedoc	Dry red	Andouillette, Chile sauce and Mexican dishes, Sausage
Fleurie, *see* Beaujolais			
Frascati Superiore	Italy	Demi-sec white	Béarnaise sauce, Fettuccine Alfredo, Soufflé with spinach
Fronsac	Bordeaux	Dry red	Black pudding, Basque chicken, Guinea fowl, Hare

WINE	REGION	WINE TYPE	FOOD
Furmint	Hungary	Dry white	Curry dishes, Goulash, Hummus, Poultry casseroles
Gaillac	Southwest France	Dry white	Crème caramel or brûlée, Grilled sardines, Mackerel with butter and spring onions, Squid cooked in their own juices
Gavi	Italy	Dry white	Creamy pasta dishes, Mushroom risotto, Oysters
Gevrey-Chambertin	Burgundy	Dry red	Coq au vin, Mint sauce, Mushroom soufflés, tarts, and risottos, Roast duck and duck à l'orange
Gewürztraminer *vendanges tardives*	Alsace		Barbecued meats, Brown sugar–based desserts, Chinese food, especially chicken or other meats in sweet-and-sour sauce, Creamed onions, Curried tomato soup, Duck à l'orange, Indian food, especially lamb curry, Pot roast, Red cabbage with apples, Roast pork in mustard sauce, Sauerbraten, Smoked fish, Thai food
Gigondas	Rhône	Dry red	Beef bourguignonne and goulash, Goose stuffed with prunes, Octopus, Osso bucco, Sausage and mash, Wild boar
Grave del Friuli	Italy	Sparkling	Light pasta dishes, especially cream or cheese based, Seafood dishes
Graves	Bordeaux	Dry red, Red	Duck à l'orange, Fish in red wine, Roast beef or steak, Steak and kidney pie
		White	Grilled scallops, Haddock, Mackerel with butter and spring onions, Veal, White wine sauce dishes
Greco di Tufo	Italy	Dry white	Anchovies or anchovy paste, Green salad, Olives and olive paste, Pasta in tomato and cheese sauce, Risotto

WINE	REGION	WINE TYPE	FOOD
Grenache	France or New World	Dry red	Andouillette and Merguez sausages, Beef casseroles, Chili con carne and other spicy meat dishes, Steak tartare
Gros Plant	Loire/ Nantes	Dry white	Avocados or guacamole, Mackerel with green gooseberry sauce and other oily fish dishes, Raw vegetables and salads, Sashimi
Grüner Veltliner	Austria	Sweet white	Chinese food, Roast pork, Wiener Schnitzel
Hermitage	Rhône	Dry red	Beef Wellington, Boeuf en daube and other red meat stews and casseroles, Grouse, Lamb shoulder
Irouléguy	Southwest France	Dry red	Barbecued meats, Basque chicken, Chorizo
Juliénas, see Beajolais			
Kékfrankos	Hungary	Dry red	Beef bourguignonne and beef Stroganoff, Moussaka, Sausage and mash
Lirac	Rhône	Red	Barbecued meats
		Rosé	Lamb chops, Tapenade
Loupiac	Bordeaux	Sweet white	Bread and butter pudding, Chestnut-, fruit-, and raspberry-based desserts, fruit salad or compote, Iles flottantes. See also Barsac, Cadillac, Monbazillac, Ste-Croix-du-Mont, Sauternes
Mâcon	Burgundy	Dry white	Cheese fondue, Fish and chips, Pasta with carbonara sauce, Roast or stuffed peppers, Salt cod with garlic, oil, and cream, Squid cooked in their own juices
Madeira	Spain	Fortified red	Almonds, walnuts, hazelnuts, and peanuts, Christmas pudding, Marzipan desserts

WINE	REGION	WINE TYPE	FOOD
Madiran	Southwest France	Dry red	Basque chicken, Pea and ham soup, Roast duck
Malbec	Argentina	Dry red	Beef Wellington, Empanadas, Roast lamb
Manzanilla Sherry	Spain	Fortified white	Almonds, walnuts, hazelnuts, and peanuts, Garlic-based sauces, Gazpacho, Olives
Margaux	Bordeaux	Dry red	Châteaubriand, Goose stuffed with prunes or other fruit, Roast lamb with mint sauce, Veal dishes
Marsanne	New World	Dry white	Coconut-based dishes, Curry dishes and curried tomato soup, White fish in creamy sauces
Mavrud	Bulgaria	Dry red	Beef Stroganoff, Goulash, hotpots and casseroles, Roast lamb with mint sauce
Médoc	Bordeaux	Dry red	Chicken chasseur, Grilled meats, Lamb dishes, Liver, Roast pork and chicken
Mercurey	Burgundy	Dry red	Charcuterie, Ham and bacon dishes, Macaroni and cheese, Sirloin steak with wild mushrooms
Merlot	Chile	Dry red	Beef Stroganoff, Beef Wellington, Bolognese sauce, Pizza and hearty pasta dishes, Confit de canard, Empanadas, Sirloin steak
Meursault	Burgundy	Dry white	Asparagus, Beef Stroganoff, Corn chowder, Creamy, buttery dishes, Eggs Benedict, Guacamole, Lobster dishes, Scallops in cream and tarragon sauce, Tripe, White sauce dishes. See also Bâtard-Montrachet
Minervois	Languedoc-Roussillon	Dry red	Andouillette grilled with mustard, Blanquette de veau, Grilled meats with garlic and herbs, Hare and rabbit, Ratatouille

WINE	REGION	WINE TYPE	FOOD
Monbazillac	Southwest France	Sweet white	Bread and butter pudding, Candied sweet potatoes, Cheesecake, Foie gras, Fruit-based desserts, Goat's and blue cheeses, Melon with Port, Pumpkin pie, Thai dishes. See also Barsac, Cadillac, Loupiac, Ste-Croix-du-Mont, Sauternes
Montepulciano d'Abruzzo	Italy	Dry red	Bolognese sauce, Pizza and pasta dishes with meat and béchamel sauce, Salami-based dishes
Montravel	Southwest France	Dry white	Baked ham with pineapple, Blue cheeses, Chinese food, Honey-based sauces and desserts, Seafood dishes
Morgon, see Beaujolais			
Moscatel de Valencia	Spain	Sweet white	Almond biscuits, Fruit-based desserts
Moulin-à-Vent, see Beaujolais			
Mourvèdre	France or New World	Dry red	Barbecued meats, Cassoulet, Cranberry sauce, Pepper sauce, Tarragon chicken, Venison with cranberry or juniper berries
Muscadet and Muscadet sur lie	Loire	Dry white	Blanquette de veau, Crab, scallops, oysters, prawn cocktail, and moules et frites, Egg dishes such as soufflés and quiches, Fishcakes, Green salad with oil and vinegar dressing, Mackerel with green gooseberry sauce and other oily fish dishes, Taramasalata, White fish dishes, White wine sauce dishes
Muscat de Beaumes-de-Venise	Rhône	Vin doux naturel	Baclava, Chocolate-based desserts, especially sachertorte, Fruit-, ginger-, and mint-based desserts, Ice cream, Stewed fruit, Waldorf salad

WINE	REGION	WINE TYPE	FOOD
Muscat de Rivesaltes	Roussillon	*Vin doux naturel*	Apricot-, cassis-, ginger-, orange-, and pineapple-based desserts, Chicken in sweet-and-sour sauce, Dried fruits such as figs and raisins, fresh grapes, Fruit compote and salad, Iles flottantes and meringues, Sweet crêpes, Tiramisu
Moscatel de Setúbal	Portugal	Sweet white	Almonds, grilled and salted, Baclava, Caramel- and chocolate-based desserts
Moscato Spumante	Italy	Sparkling	Fruit-based desserts, fruit compote and salad, Caramel- and chocolate-based desserts
Naoussa	Greece	Dry red	Eggplant puree, Greek food, especially kleftiko and moussaka
Navarra	Spain	Dry red	Chorizo, Couscous
Nemea	Greece	Dry red	Eggplant puree, Greek food, especially kleftiko and moussaka
Oloroso Sherry	Spain	Fortified white	Christmas pudding, Nut cakes, Praline and chocolate ice cream, Treacle and chocolate puddings
Orvieto	Italy	Dry or semi-sweet white	Creamy pasta dishes, Grilled sardines, Indian food with spicy yogurt sauces, Light fish dishes, Tempura
Pacherenc du Vic-Bilh	Southwest France	Dry to sweet white	Bread and butter pudding, Cheesecake, Chutney, Goose stuffed with prunes or other fruit, Mille feuilles, Mince pies, Pineapple-based desserts, Pipperade, Smoked ham, Tripe
Palette	Provence	Red	Aioli, Tapenade. *See also* Bandol
		Rosé	Andouillette grilled with mustard
		White	Creamed onions, Grilled or roast vegetables

WINE	REGION	WINE TYPE	FOOD
Passito	Italy	Sweet white	Ice cream, Italian biscuits or shortbread, Tiramisu
Patrimonio	Corsica	Red	Cheese fondue, Kebabs, Osso bucco, Tapenade
		White	Salade niçoise, Sardines and anchovies, Taramasalata
Pauillac	Bordeaux	Dry red	Guinea hen, pigeon, and quail, Lamb, Red meat stews and casseroles
Penedès	Spain	Dry red, Red	Empanadas, Goulash
		White	Paella, Spanish omelette with potatoes, garlic, and oil
Periquita	Portugal	Dry red	Chicken piri-piri, Kleftiko, Oxtail, Red meat stews and casseroles, Roast pork
Pineau de Charentes	Cognac	*Vin de liqueur*	Apple-, chocolate-, and cognac-based desserts, Foie gras, Melon with port, Sorbets
Pinot Blanc	Alsace	Dry white	Choucroute garnie, Eggs Benedict, cheese omelette, and other egg dishes, Kedgeree, Onion tart, Raw vegetables and salads, Savory crêpes
Pinot Grigio	Italy	Dry white	Fish and chips and other fried fish dishes, Guacamole, Hummus, Pasta with clam sauce or spring vegetables, Prosciutto, Raw vegetables, Risotto alla Milanese, Stir-fries
Pinot Gris	Alsace	Dry white	Caviar, Chicken curry, Clam chowder, Corn on the cob, Gougère, Omelette with bacon and quiche lorraine, Onion tart, Pork chops and roast pork, Raclette, Roast or stuffed peppers, Satay, Veal dishes

WINE	REGION	WINE TYPE	FOOD
Pinot Gris *(continued)*			
		Vendanges tardives	Foie gras, Kougelhopf, Sweet-and-sour sauce, White wine sauce dishes
Pinot Noir	Alsace	Dry red	Cold salmon, Potato salad, Quail, Sauerbraten
	California, Pacific Northwest, and New World		Bacon and baked ham, Bagels with salmon and cream cheese, Brussels sprouts and green vegetables, Coq au vin and chicken in cream and morel sauce, Lamb curry, Meat loaf, Pork chops, Rabbit, Roast chicken. See *also* red Burgundy appellations
Pinotage	South Africa	Dry red	Beef Wellington, Chili con carne, Chorizo, Couscous, Moussaka, Pea and ham soup, Pigeon, Roast beef and steak
Pomerol	Bordeaux	Dry red	Beef and steak dishes, Chicken in sweet-and-sour sauce, Goose stuffed with prunes or other fruit, Grilled lamb chops, Mint sauce and pepper sauce, Partridge and pheasant, Roast duck, Shepherd's pie, Truffles, black and white, Wild boar
Pommard	Burgundy	Dry red	Cajun-style meats, Confit de canard, Kidneys, Pepper sauce, Roast duck and roast lamb with mint sauce, Wild boar
Port	Portugal	Fortified red	Almonds, walnuts, hazelnuts, and peanuts, Chocolate-based desserts, Melon and Port, Mince pies
Pouilly-Fumé	Loire	Dry white	Eels with a creamy herb sauce, Goat's cheese, Grilled carp, Jambon persillé, Moules marinières, oysters, and seafood pizza, Paella, Tripe, Vinaigrette sauce. See *also* Sauvignon Blanc and Sancerre

WINE	REGION	WINE TYPE	FOOD
Pouilly-Fuissé	Burgundy	Dry white	Cold salmon, Grilled bass, Fish terrines, Quiches and soufflés, Japanese food
Poulsard	Arbois	Dry red	Game, Jambalaya, Kleftiko, Spicy meat dishes
Puligny-Montrachet	Burgundy	Dry white	Caviar, Creamy and buttery sauces, Lobster, Monkfish, Roast veal
Quarts de Chaume	Loire	Sweet white	Chocolate-based desserts, Exotic fruit-based desserts and fruit salads, Kougelhopf
Regaleali Rosato	Italy	Dry rosé	Roast or stuffed peppers
Regnié, see Beaujolais			
Reguengos	Portugal	Dry red	Carpaccio, Chicken piri-piri
Retsina	Greece	Dry white	Eggplant dishes, Olives and anchovies, Spicy sausages
Richebourg	Burgundy	Dry red	Calves' liver, Coffee-based desserts, Grouse, venison, and roast meats
Riesling	Alsace	Dry white	Blanquette de veau, Boudin blanc (white pudding), Bouillabaisse, Chicken in cream and morel sauce, Creamed onions, Horse-radish sauce, Mustard sauce, Olives, Potato salad or creamy potato dishes, Quiche lorraine, Raspberry-based desserts, Seafood in creamy sauces and moules marinières, Smoked salmon, White fish dishes
		Vendanges tardives	Acras, Chinese food, Smoked ham, Waldorf salad
Riesling	Germany	Dry to sweet white	
		Kabinett	Béarnaise sauce, Cranberry sauce, Gravlax, Sashimi and sushi

WINE	REGION	WINE TYPE	FOOD
Riesling *(continued)*			
		Spätlese	Chinese food, Roast pork with mustard sauce, Smoked ham, Tomato salad
		Auslese	Brown sugar–based desserts, Duck a l'orange, Foie gras, Red cabbage with apples, Smoked fish
		Beerenauslese	Cherry-based desserts, Sacher-torte and other chocolate-based desserts
Riesling	New World	Dry white	Apple-based desserts, Choucroute garnie, Curry dishes, Japanese food, Pike with garlic and poached white fish dishes
Rioja	Spain	Red	Beef potpie, Curried tomato soup, Greek food, especially moussaka, Lamb, Liver, Merguez sausage, Roast pork
		Rosé	Paella
		White	Octopus, Roasted, spicy sausages, Salt cod balls, Stuffed onions, Tapas
Rosso Cònero	Italy	Red	Bolognese sauce dishes, Duck a l'orange, Salami and spicy meats
		Rosé	Cured meats, Saltimbocca alla Romana and other veal dishes, Roast lamb
Rueda	Spain	Dry white	Salads, Sausages, dried or smoked, Spicy meat casseroles, Grilled or roast vegetables
Rully	Burgundy	Red	Charcuterie, Coq au vin, Roast pork, Escargots à la Bourguignonne
		White	Artichokes, Caesar salad, Jambon persillé, Savory crêpes, Smoked salmon, Satay, Soufflés with broccoli and cheese

WINE	REGION	WINE TYPE	FOOD
St-Amour, see Beaujolais			
St-Emilion	Bordeaux	Dry red	Beef potpie, Beef Wellington, Chicken curry, Confit de canard, Game and venison, Lamb with herbes de provence, Pasta with pesto sauce, Pheasant, pigeon, and quail, Pot roast, Pot-au-feu, Roast meats such as chicken, turkey, and beef, Sausage
St-Estèphe	Bordeaux	Dry red	Lamb with flageolets or light meat casseroles, Rabbit, Roast lamb
St-Georges-St-Emilion, see St-Emilion			
St-Joseph	Rhone	Dry red	Boiled or roast vegetables, Grilled meats, Kebabs, Melon with Parma ham. See also Syrah, Cornas, Côte Rôtie, Crozes-Hermitage
St-Julien	Bordeaux	Dry red	Lamb crown roast, Roast turkey with traditional trimmings. See also St-Estèphe
St-Véran	Burgundy	Dry white	Artichokes, Asparagus in vinaigrette sauce, Herring, Soufflés with spinach and cheese, Steak tartare
Ste-Croix-du-Mont	Southwest France	Sweet white	Cheeses, Foie gras and other pâtés, Fruit salad and orange-based desserts. See also Barsac, Cadillac, Loupiac, Monbazillac, Sauternes
Samos	Greece	Sweet white	Baclava, Nuts, almonds, and honey-based desserts, Pastries and breads
Sancerre	Loire/Centre	Dry white	Avocado, Béarnaise sauce, Creole and teriyaki chicken, Hollandaise sauce and mustard sauce, Omelettes, Fishcakes, Poached, steamed, or lightly grilled salmon, Sashimi and sushi, Seafood dishes, especially smoked eels, Taramasalata, Tomato sauce dishes, Vichyssoise, Wiener Schnitzel. See also Sauvignon Blanc–France

WINE	REGION	WINE TYPE	FOOD
Sangiovese	California	Dry red	Brasciola and carpaccio, Pasta dishes with meat and béchamel sauce, Pizza bolognese, Saltimbocca alla Romana. See also Brunello di Montalcino
Saumur and Saumur-Champigny	Loire	Dry red	Anchovies or anchovy paste, Baked ham with pineapple, Beef bourguignonne, Confit de canard, Grilled lamb chops, Lemon chicken, Meat fondue, Quail, Raspberry- and strawberry-based desserts
Sauternes	Bordeaux	Sweet white	Bread and butter pudding, Brown sugar–based desserts, Cheeses, especially blue cheeses, Chocolate-, Cointreau-, and lemon-based desserts, Christmas pudding, Crème caramel or brûlée, Foie gras, Pecan pie, Tiramisu, Waldorf salad
Sauvignon Blanc	France		Artichokes, Avocado, Ceviche, Egg dishes, soufflés, and quiches, Fish and chips, Jambon persillé, Pike with garlic, Grilled carp or haddock, Pizza with seafood, Prawn cocktail and other seafood dishes, especially scallops in cream and tarragon sauce, Smoked eels, Stir-fries, Thai food, White fish dishes, White wine sauce dishes. See also Sancerre and Pouilly-Fumé
	New World		Asparagus, Chicken creole, Chicken piri-piri and teriyaki chicken, Chicken salad, Fishcakes and prawns, Gazpacho, Ginger-based desserts, Jambalaya, Pasta with spring vegetables, Salsa, red and green, and other tomato-based sauces, Sashimi, Stir-fries, Tomato salad and raw vegetables
Sauvignon Colli Orientali del Friuli	Italy	Dry white	Mozzarella and Ricotta cheeses, Prawns, scampi, and seafood pasta dishes. See also Sauvignon Blanc

WINE	REGION	WINE TYPE	FOOD
Savennières	Loire	Dry white	Creole chicken, Goat's cheese, Grilled scallops. See also Chenin Blanc
Savigny-Les-Beaune	Burgundy	Dry red	Chicken chasseur, Lamb curry, Mushroom and red wine sauces, Tarragon chicken. See also Pinot Noir
Sémillon	New World	Dry white	Barbecued and blackened fish, Blue cheeses, Chicken chasseur, Chinese food, Coconut-based desserts and savory dishes, Ham and pork dishes, Honey-based dishes, Indian food with spicy yogurt sauces, Mackerel with butter and spring onions and other oily fish dishes, Monkfish and other seafood, Pumpkin pie, Spicy white meat dishes
Sherry, see Amontillado, Fino, Manzanilla, or Oloroso			
Shiraz	Australia	Dry red	Barbecued meats, Bean and pasta soup, Boeuf en daube, cassoulet, and other red meat stews and casseroles, Chicken paprika and southern fried chicken, Chili con carne and chile sauce, Couscous, Cranberry sauce, Duck à l'orange, Game, Greek food, Hamburgers, Horseradish sauce, Lamb curry, Meat fondue, Merguez sausages, Pepper sauce, Sirloin steak, Stuffed cabbage, Toad-in-the-hole, Venison and wild boar
Soave	Italy	Dry white	Aioli, Bruschetta, Chef's salad and other salads, Gazpacho, Macaroni and cheese, Pasta with pesto sauce, Prawns, seafood salad, and light, white fish dishes, Risotto alla Milanese, Teriyaki chicken

WINE	REGION	WINE TYPE	FOOD
Sylvaner	Alsace	Dry white	Anchovies or anchovy paste, Chicken in sweet-and-sour sauce, Croque monsieur or madame, Onion tarts, Pike with garlic, Quiche lorraine, Salt cod with garlic, oil, and cream, Sweetbreads
Syrah	New World	Dry red	Cajun-style and barbecued meats, Game, Mushroom and red wine sauces. *See also* Hermitage, Cornas, Côte Rôtie, Crozes-Hermitage, St-Joseph
Tavel	Rhône	Dry rosé	Anchovies or anchovy paste, Asparagus in vinaigrette sauce, Bouillabaisse, Onion tart, Salami-based dishes
Tempranillo, *see* Rioja			
Tokàji	Hungary	Sweet white	Carrot cake, Christmas pudding, Thai food. *See also* Muscat de Beaumes-de-Venise, Ste-Croix-du-Mont, Sauternes
Trebbiano d'Abruzzo/ Ugni Blanc	Italy or New World	Dry white	Egg dishes with ham or bacon, Creamy spinach and pasta dishes, Risotto alla Milanese
Vacqueyras	Rhône	Dry red	Beef Stroganoff, Escargots à la Bourguinonne, Pigeon. *See also* Grenache
Valdepeñas	Spain	Dry red	Squid cooked in their own juices
Valpolicella Classico	Italy	Dry red	Brasciola, Italian garlic and tomato dishes, Mexican food, Mushroom risotto, Osso bucco, Proscuitto, Raclette, Tuna salad

WINE	REGION	WINE TYPE	FOOD
Verdicchio	Italy	Dry white	Antipasti, Fish and chips and other fried fish dishes, Light, creamy pasta dishes, Moules et frites, Seafood salad and other seafood dishes
Vernaccia di San Gimignano	Italy	Dry white	Bouillabaisse, Bruschetta, Grilled white fish, especially bass, Pesto-based pasta dishes
Vin de Corse	Corsica	Red	Boeuf en daube, Corn bread, Eggplant, Merguez sausages, Polenta
		White	Bouillabaisse, Tabbouleh, Tuna salad
Vin de Paille	Jura	*Vin doux naturel*	Apple- and apricot-based desserts, Foie gras, Sweet crêpes, Thai food. *See also* Pacherenc du Vic-Bilh, Tokàji
Vinho Verde	Portugal	Dry white	Ceviche, Chicken piri-piri, Green salad with oil and vinegar dressing, Grilled sardines, Mackerel with green gooseberry sauce, Salsas, red and green, Vinaigrette sauce
Vino Nobile de Montepulciano	Italy	Dry red	Roast lamb with mint sauce, Red meat stews and casseroles, Wild boar. *See also* Brunello di Montalcino, Sangiovese
Viognier	Rhône, Italy, or New World	Dry white	Artichokes, Carrot soup, Chef's salad, Curry, Gazpacho, Indian food. *See also* Condrieu
Volnay	Burgundy	Dry red	Mushroom and red wine dishes, Quail, Rabbit, Roast beef, Veal dishes. *See also* Echezeaux
Vosne-Romanée	Burgundy	Dry red	Brown sugar–based desserts, Coffee-based desserts, Game, Roast turkey with traditional trimmings, Truffles, black and white.

WINE	REGION	WINE TYPE	FOOD
Vouvray	Loire	Dry to sweet white	Acras, Apple-, fruit-, and lemon-based desserts, Béarnaise and hollandaise sauce, Goat's cheese, Goose stuffed with prunes or other fruit, Quiches and soufflés, Sweet-and-sour sauce, White fish dishes. See also Chenin Blanc
		Sparkling (mousseux)	Apple-, fruit-, and lemon-based desserts, Mince pies, Sweet crêpes
Weissburgunder	Germany	Dry red	Braised beef, stews, and casseroles, Roast pork, Wiener Schnitzel
Zinfandel	California	Red	Eggplant-based dishes, Baked beans, Barbecued meats, Beef potpie, Beef tacos, Buffalo wings, Cajun-style meats, Cassoulet, Chicken paprika, Chili con carne, Chorizo sausage, Empanadas, Goulash, Greek food, Hamburgers, Meat loaf, Pepper sauce, Pizza bolognese, Ratatouille, Roast duck, Roast turkey with traditional trimmings, Salads, Sausage and mash, Venison with cranberries or juniper berries
		White	Grilled white fish, Pasta dishes, Octopus, Roast vegetables
Zitsa	Greece	Dry white	Anchovies, Hummus, Olives, Spicy sausages, Tapas

Wine Vocabulary

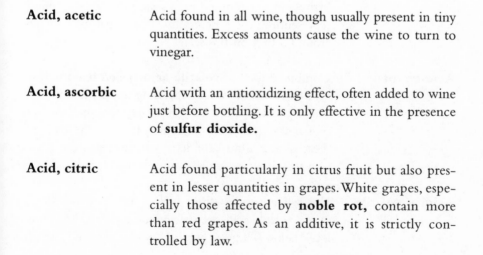

Acid, acetic   Acid found in all wine, though usually present in tiny quantities. Excess amounts cause the wine to turn to vinegar.

Acid, ascorbic   Acid with an antioxidizing effect, often added to wine just before bottling. It is only effective in the presence of **sulfur dioxide.**

Acid, citric   Acid found particularly in citrus fruit but also present in lesser quantities in grapes. White grapes, especially those affected by **noble rot,** contain more than red grapes. As an additive, it is strictly controlled by law.

Acid, lactic   Acid that appears during the **malolactic fermenta-tion** of the wine when **malic acid** changes into car-bon dioxide and lactic acid. Eventually this fades and becomes imperceptible in tasting.

Acid, malic   Once the grape ripens, the malic acid present at high levels in the green grapes decreases. Its tart taste of green apples makes it easily recognizable. The hotter the year, the faster it decreases during the ripening process, which is why it is more apparent when the weather has been colder.

Acid, tartaric   Regarded as the most noble acid, tartaric acid has more acidifying power than the other acids contained in wine, and is not commonly found in fruits other than grapes. The tartaric acid content goes down as the grape ripens, then varies depending on the weather.

Acidify   To add lemon juice or vinegar to a sauce or cooked dish.

Acidity, fixed   The total of all the acids contained in the fruit itself, such as **tartaric acid, malic acid, lactic acid.**

Acidity, real   Intensity of acidity, usually expressed in **pH** (potential hydrogen), is expressed on a scale from 0 to 7, with 7 representing total neutrality. The usual pH ranges around 3 to 4 on this scale.

Acidity, total   Combined total of **volatile acidity** and **fixed acidi-ty.** This naturally varies depending upon whether sea-sons are cold (when the grapes are too acid) or hot (when the grapes are overripe). It is on the basis of these figures and of the legal standards that the deci-sion to acidify or to disacidify a wine is made.

Acidity, volatile   In small quantities (from 0.3 to 0.4 gram per liter), excess volatile acids are strictly controlled by law. Only levels below 0.9 gram per liter (production) and 1 gram per liter (retail trade) are tolerated; quantities higher than this make the wine too sour. This acidity, mainly made up of **acetic acid,** increases as the wine ages.

Acidulation

Adding acid to wine made from grapes deficient in natural acid in order to bring the wine into balance. Acidulation is legal in California (where the warmer climates keep acid levels down) but illegal in France. It is interesting to note that adding sugar **(chaptalization)** is legal in France but illegal in California.

Aioli

A Mediterranean mayonnaise made with garlic, egg yolks, and oil.

Al dente

A term used for describing the perfect texture of cooked pasta: tender but still slightly firm to the bite. As each type of pasta (lasagne, fettuccine, penne, tagliatelli, rigatoni, fusilli, and so on) demands a different cooking time, it is essential to test pasta regularly during its preparation.

Alcohol

An essential element in wine, alcohol is produced during fermentation, when enzymes created by the yeasts change the sugar content of the grape juice into alcohol, carbon dioxide, and heat. The level of alcohol varies from under 7 degrees to more than 15 degrees in wine. To obtain 1 degree of alcohol, 18 grams of sugar must be added per liter for white wines, and 17 grams per liter for red.

Anthocyanin

The red pigments in grapes, which give red wine its color. The purple-red color of young wine is almost exclusively caused by fairly unstable anthocyanin molecules that, in the course of aging, join up with **tannins** to give the wine its ruby red color. This **polymerization** of tannin and anthocyanin is helped by the dissolution of oxygen in the wine, which produces stable polymers.

Appellation   The geographic origin of a wine, not synonymous with the term *terroir.*

AOC   *Appellation d'origine contrôlée,* a designation created by the French authorities to establish specific areas of production, grape varieties, minimum levels of sugar in the must and of alcohol in the wine, maximum yield per acre, pruning of the vine, and cultivation and vinification methods.

Aromas   These are the scents that a wine gives off, as absorbed by the taster's nose and palate. Three levels of aromas can be distinguished: primary, or varietal aromas; secondary aromas resulting from the fermentation; and tertiary aromas, which develop as the wine ages. Together they form the wine's **bouquet.**

Aromatic esters   The compounds formed most often during fermentation by the wine's acids and alcohols.

Au gratin   The cooking term used for dishes that are browned in the oven or under a grill. Gratins are often made with béchamel sauce, cheese, or eggs.

Auslese   German white wines made from late-harvest grapes with a high sugar concentration.

Balance   The harmony between the various elements of a wine, such as acidity, sweetness, alcohol, and tannin content.

Barrel fermented   Wine that is fermented in oak barrels as opposed to stainless-steel tanks.

Barrique   A French term for a barrel, the capacity of which may vary from one region to another: In the Bordeaux area, where it is most commonly used, it contains 225 liters (four *barriques* make one *tonneau*); in the Muscadet area, it contains 228 liters; while in Touraine-Anjou, it holds 232 liters. The traditional English equivalent is the hogshead. In France, other names are used depending on the region and capacity.

Beerenauslese
QmP

German wines made from grapes affected by *Botrytis cinerea,* or **noble rot.**

Blanc, Blanco,
Branco

French, Spanish, Portuguese for white.

Blanc de Blancs

"White of whites," meaning a white wine made of white grapes, such as Champagne made from Chardonnay. It is also used as the names of some wineries' special blends of still white wines, ranging from dry to medium dry.

Blanc de Noirs

White wine made from red or black grapes.

Bleeding

The bleeding process, or *saignée,* consists in drawing off some of the wine during fermentation. The light-colored wine drawn off is used to make rosé wines such as **Clairet** in Bordeaux and Clarete in Rioja.

Blending

Blending, or *assemblage,* is the mixing of several vats of wine varieties to make a more balanced wine and is usually performed after each variety has fermented individually. For example, Bordeaux are usually a blend of Cabernet Sauvignon, Cabernet Franc, and Merlot.

Bodega

An agricultural estate in Spain. However, wines labeled Bodega do not necessarily contain grapes that all come from the estate in question.

Body

Used to describe a wine with good tannic structure and good aging potential.

Botrytis

A mold that attacks grapes, it manifests itself either as **gray rot,** which may then endanger the harvest; or, in certain atmospheric conditions, as **noble rot,** which is used to make dessert wines such as Sauternes, Barsac, Monbazillac, certain Anjou wines, German wines like Auslese, Beerenauslese, or Trockenbeerenauslese, and the famous Hungarian Tokàji.

Botrytis cinerea

Literally "noble rot," *edelfäule* in German, which dehydrates grapes left late on the vine and concentrates their juice.

Bottle sickness

Unbalance of wine flavor after bottling or after rough travel, caused by excessive aeration; clears up when wine is allowed to rest.

Bouche

The French word for mouth is used to describe the body and impressions of the wine when tasting.

Bouquet

Complex emanation from a wine, perceptible in the nose, resulting from maturation and oak aging. Bouquet is more complex than and encompasses **aroma,** which is present only with young wines.

Brettanomyces

An undesirable yeast found on grapes, and therefore in wines, which produces very disagreeable odors when in excess and which is a sign of poor hygiene in the winery. In small amounts it escapes unnoticed, or shows itself as an earthy, manurelike smell we sometimes appreciate.

Broker

See **Courtier.**

Brut

A French term for sparkling wines, it indicates very low level of sugar (up to 15 grams per liter). There is no sugar present in *brut Intégral* or *brut zéro* Champagne.

Capers

The unopened flower buds of the Mediterranean caper bush, a sort of creeper. They are pickled in vinegar and used as a seasoning.

Carbonic maceration

The type of vinification during which red wine grapes are put into vats as they are, without being crushed. This used to be a natural process, with the grapes being left to ferment without interference. Now the vat is closed and filled with carbon dioxide, which causes the **malic acid** to break down and intracellular fermentations to take place, changing part of the sugar into alcohol. A few days later, the free-run wine is drained off to be blended at a later stage with the **press wine**. The **alcoholic fermentation** is then allowed to finish. This process has proved particularly effective for Gamay wines, such as the Beaujolais Primeurs, that are sold and consumed when young.

Chaptalization

Named for its founder Chaptal, this technique consists of adding sugar (cane, beet, or rectified, concentrated must) to the **must** before fermentation to give the wine a higher alcoholic content. It is strictly forbidden in many countries and is usually controlled by law in those countries that permit it (in France a maximum of three kilos of sugar per hectoliter of grape juice is allowed). The new EU regulations have added to this legislation, defining certain parameters: Chaptalization should be authorized only under certain conditions relative to the degree of ripeness, the climatic conditions, and the production methods used. Chaptalization is a necessary evil in difficult years; however, in France it has become something of a habit, allowing growers to harvest maximum volume in the sure knowledge that they can boost the degree of alcohol by chaptalizing. The EU would like French growers to use only rectified concentrated musts, or RCMs, when chaptalizing. Today, new appliances are used to detect fraudulent chaptalization by nuclear magnetic resonance.

Château   To the northwest of Bordeaux, in the Médoc, most country residences have vineyards that have become famous. As a result, the term has come to designate the wine from a particular estate. A real château does not necessarily stand on every property.

Clairet   Light red wine obtained by **bleeding** in the course of fermentation of red wine. Not to be confused with **Claret.**

Claret   The British name for the red wines of Bordeaux.

Climat   French term originating in Burgundy to indicate a legally defined geographical area. It has nothing to do with weather. However, different *climats* can have varying weather climates in them or between them.

Clos   A French term that originally referred to a vine-growing parcel of land surrounded by a wall, particularly in Burgundy. Many of the original walls even in the oldest properties are still standing.

Cold stabilization   A method of clarifying wine by lowering its temperature to thirty-two degrees Fahrenheit for a short period, allowing the suspended particles to drop out.

Complex   The term used to describe a wine that has many different levels and layers of flavors and textures.

Concentrated   The term used to describe a wine that has a lot of extracted matter, and is intense and rich. The extract is comprised of the nonvolatile solids of a wine: sugars, acids, minerals, phenolics, glycerol, and so on.

Corked   The expression used for a wine that has a very strong smell of rotten cork. The wine is usually undrinkable. This rather rare occurrence is caused by the development of molds on the cork.

Courtier

A courtier or broker is an intermediary between the grower and the *négociant.*

Cru

Literally, in French, a "growth" or tract of land such as a vineyard, the term is principally used to mean a vineyard's rank in the 1855 classification or ranking of Bordeaux vineyards and their wines into five classes or Crus. Eighty-three Médoc, Graves, and Sauternes châteaux were thus classified in 1855, but since then hundreds more around Bordeaux have classified themselves as first to fifth Crus or as Crus Exceptionnels or as Crus Bourgeois (the lesser-quality categories preceding the Crus).

Crush

The physical act of crushing the grapes, as well as the term referring to the harvest season.

Cuvaison, Cuvage

The French term for the essential stage in the making of a wine, from when the **musts** from the harvest are put into the fermentation vats, up to the draining off or *égouttage.*

Cuve

A vat designed to hold the fermenting **musts,** or to store wines. Some vats are closed with an upper lid fitted with a hatch, as in Bordeaux; others are open, as in Burgundy. The vats are made of various materials: Wooden vats were once used, but nowadays stainless-steel vats are preferred for cleanliness and, principally, temperature control.

Cuvée

A French term literally meaning "vatful," the word signifies a specific selection of wine that may or may not have been blended. See **Blending.**

Daube

A method of cooking meat, usually beef, which braises the meat in a red wine sauce, often with garden vegetables and seasonings.

Decanting   The process of separating the sediment of a wine from the clear liquid. During the decanting operation a young wine comes into contact with the air, so that the addition of oxygen makes it more palatable. Should the wine be too old, such an operation can be disastrous, as it accelerates the process of deterioration.

Declassification   When a wine exceeds certain norms (in terms of yield), or falls short (in degree of alcohol), the wine is declassified and loses its **AOC** classification. The decision may be taken voluntarily by the winemaker. Such wine may be used to make vinegar or pure alcohol.

Dekkera   The spore-producing form of the yeast genus brettanomyces.

Demi-sec   EU classification for white wines with a sugar content of less than nine grams per liter. In Champagnes, it is one category below **sec** in terms of dryness, and considered the ideal accompaniment to dessert pastries.

Deposit   The sediment of solid particles found in wine that separate from the wine during fermentation and aging. In the case of white wines, these are often fragments of colorless crystalline deposits; in red wines, they are usually a combination of **tannins** and pigments. See **Decanting.**

Dessert wine   US legal term for wines of more than 14 percent but not more than 24 percent alcoholic strength by volume; includes appetizer wines such as Sherry.

Distillation   The operation during which the alcohol is separated by heating the alcoholic mixture, on the principle that alcohol has a boiling point lower than that of water: The first vapors to be given off are alcoholic ones that are condensed by cooling.

DO   *Denominacion de origen;* the Spanish equivalent of the French **AOC.**

DOC   *Denominazione di origine controllata;* the Italian equivalent of the French **AOC.** The classification underwrites the origin of the wine, but not necessarily the quality. There are more than 220 at present.

Doce, Dolce, Dulce   "Sweet" in Portuguese, Italian, Spanish.

DOCG   *Denominazione di origine controllata garantita.* An Italian guarantee that refers to testing by sensory analysis. Existing ones are Barbaresco, Barolo, Brunello, Chianti, and Vino Nobile di Montepulciano.

Dry   Something of a misnomer. In the case of Champagne, it in fact means "sweet"; the driest Champagnes are actually called **brut** or **extra dry.**

Earthy   The positive characteristics of loamy topsoil, mushrooms, or truffles sometimes found in red wines.

Elevage   Literally "raising," this French term describes the operations of maturing and blending young wines to attain better balance.

En primeur   Rather than being sold when it is ready to drink, wine is most often offered at a much earlier stage. In Bordeaux, the Grands Crus usually sell all or part of a year's harvest (usually in September) the following March or April, in what are known as sales *en primeur.*

Enology, Oenology   The science and study of winemaking.

Espumoso, Espumante   Spanish and Portuguese for sparkling wine, such as Champagne.

Estate bottled   This originally meant that the wine was produced and bottled entirely at the winery adjoining the proprietor's vineyard, but amendments have broadened it to include any vineyards controlled by the same proprietor or owned by members of a cooperative winery within the same delimited viticultural area as the winery.

Esters   Volatile bodies resulting from the combination of an alcohol and an organic acid. They do not have such a marked influence on the wine's **bouquet** as is commonly thought.

Extra dry   The quality of sparkling or still wine containing between 12 and 20 grams of sugar per liter.

Fermentation, alcoholic   Transformation of the sugar contained in the **must** into alcohol and carbon dioxide, in the presence of yeasts.

Fermentation, malolactic   This follows the **alcoholic fermentation.** Malic acid is affected by specific bacteria and changed into **lactic acid** and carbon dioxide. Because lactic acid is less harsh than malic acid, the wine becomes softer and more pleasant to drink than when young.

Fining   Fining, or *collage,* is a way of clearing wines before they are bottled. In this method, a colloid is added to the wine to absorb suspended particles and to fall to the bottom of the container. Products used are beaten egg white, fish glue, casein, or bentonite, a type of clay. The wine is then drawn off and sometimes filtered before bottling.

Flintstone   This evokes the smell of two flints being rubbed together, characteristic of Pouilly-Fumé in the Loire Valley and some other wines, usually made from the Sauvignon grape.

Fortified   Said of a wine to which wine spirit (brandy) has been added, such as Port or Sherry.

Foxy   In general, this term describes wine with an unpleasant and aggressively gamey smell. Specifically, it refers to the red Concord grape, native of North America and belonging to the *Vitis labrusca* species. (Grapes from *V. vinifera* are the best for winemaking—and indeed, all those varieties with which we are familiar are *V. vinifera*.)

Fruity   A characteristic of a young wine, or of a wine that has retained its fruity aromas.

Glycerin   A trialcohol with a slightly sweet flavor, one of the important constituents of wine. On the palate it is often more pronounced in wines matured in new oak.

Gnocchi   Italian potato, egg, and flour dumplings.

Grassy   Aromas and flavors resembling new-mown grass, a negative characteristic when dominant.

Graves   Soils made up of gravels and drift boulders. Graves is also one of the seven major Bordeaux appellations, named this because of its soil type.

Gray rot   *See* **Rot, gray.**

Green   Used to describe a wine with excessive fruit acidity, especially if it has a malic (applelike) aroma.

Hectoliter   One hundred liters, the equivalent of 22 imperial or 26.5 U.S. gallons. In the EU, wine production is referred to in hectoliters per hectare (hl/ha).

Herbaceous   Aromas and flavors that are reminiscent of herbs or the leafy and branchy parts of the plant. They are not desirable if they are too strong.

Hybrid	A cross between two species of vine. As a result of the **phylloxera** crisis and the subsequent crossings of American and European species, phylloxera-resistant hybrids have been produced. Such hybrids have not been encouraged, because the quality of the wine has tended to be mediocre.
Jammy	In red wines, this describes the taste of ripe fruitiness combined with natural berrylike flavours. If too jammy it is an indication that the wine was partly fermented or that the grapes matured too quickly in a hot climate.
Kabinett	High-quality German dry white wines **(QmP)** that are never **chaptalized.**
Larousse Gastronomique	The wine and food lover's bible by Prosper Montagné—a gastronomic encyclopedia more than filled with eighty-five hundred recipes and one thousand illustrations, providing not only practical recipes, but also a history of cooking, anecdotes, and explanations with sources from Rabelais, Brillat-Savarin, August Escoffier, and more. The first French edition was published in 1938; the first English translation in 1961. It is truly a great read and an indispensable tool.
Lees	Made up of yeasts in a latent state, **tartaric acid,** and other residual matter from the harvest, the lees form a dark yellowy deposit at the bottom of the cask. They are removed during **racking.**
Madeirized	A term meaning "oxidized" or "baked," such as by the heat-treatment method practiced in Madeira and some other countries. It can also refer to a white wine that has oxidized badly and browned in color, usually because of poor storage and/or excessive age. The phenomenon takes its name from the taste of Madeira, and is due to the presence of harmful levels of ethyl aldehyde.
Malic	Applelike aroma of malic acid from incompletely ripened grapes.

Marc   The solid parts of the grape, obtained after pressing, forming a cake that is sometimes used for distillation in two different processes: The marc can be sprayed with water and drained off before distillation, or it can be placed in special stills into which steam is forced. The resulting spirit is called *eau de vie de marc,* or just marc for short. In Champagne, the term is the loading unit for the press, corresponding to four thousand kilos of grapes.

Marinate   Food (usually meats) are marinated in marinades to tenderize them and to impart flavor. The marinade is usually of an oil base with an acidic element such as lemon, vinegar, or soy sauce.

Maturation   The maturation of a wine is the function of its composition, its origin *(terroir),* and its vintage. No one knows for certain what happens during the aging process. We know that there is an olfactive evolution, or a change from simple aromas to a complex bouquet. During bottle aging, red wines deposit little plaques, grains of coloring agents, and other molecules, which bond and fall to the bottom of the bottle. The heavier clusters settle faster than the smaller ones, which need years to settle. As these coloring agents settle in the bottles, the intensity of the wine's color diminishes, becoming more and more reddish brick, and finally yellowish, as the **anthocyanins,** or coloring agents, in the **tannins** soften and diminish as the tannins do. **Polymerization** progresses continually as the wine ages so that tannic wines for long aging become gradually harder and more tannic before reaching a peak where they are more tannic than when they were in the barrel. Then the slope starts a gradual decline. The extra-large molecules lose their ability to combine with other proteins, and their astringency diminishes. At the same time they are combining with other components in the wine, becoming insoluble and precipitating to form the characteristic deposit. At this point the wine is in its mature, mellow phase and is softer, richer, and rounder: This is maturity.

Mercaptan

From the Latin for capturing mercury, a chemical term referring to the skunklike compounds formed by yeast reacting with the sulfur in the **lees** after the primary **alcoholic fermentation.**

Méthode champenoise

The originality of this way of making sparkling wines lies in the creation of effervescence in the bottle. The wines used have completed their fermentations (alcoholic and sometimes malolactic) and are what the Champenois call "clear wines," to which *liqueur de tirage,* made up of sugar solution and yeasts, is added. This provokes a second **alcoholic fermentation** in the bottle, which is carefully closed with a metal capsule (or cork). This fermentation produces carbon dioxide, which is trapped in the bottle and mixes into the wine; this is how the effervescence is formed. The bottles are then stored in a cellar *sur lattes* (upon slats of wood) until they are released onto the market (they can be kept for several years in this way without detracting from their freshness).

When the wines are being prepared for shipping, the deposits of dead yeasts that have fallen by force of gravity to the lower side of the bottle are removed. The operation involves raising the bottle progressively onto *pupitres* (racks) and giving it a quarter turn daily **(riddling)** so that the deposit forms against the cork. Today this traditional way of making Champagne is often replaced by an automatic mechanical operation using *giropallets,* which gives excellent results. The bottles come out neck-down and with the deposit collected against the cork. The neck is immersed in a saline solution that freezes a few fluid ounces of the wine, forming a plug of ice that includes the deposit.

The capsule is then removed in the stage known as *dégorgement* (disgorging). A *liqueur d'expédition* is then added; this is a mixture of old wine, pure spirit (or cognac), citric acid when necessary, anhydride sulfite, and, most important, a sugar solution in quantities that will determine the designation: **brut** (from 0 to 15 grams), **extra dry** (from 12 to 15 grams), **sec** (from 17 to 35 grams), **demi-sec** (from 33 to 50 grams). The bottle can then be corked, wired, and labeled.

Microclimate
An area where the soil, combined with other environmental factors, produces a distinctive wine. The more American term for the French *climat.*

Mildew
A parasitic mold that attacks the green parts of the vine. It used to be treated with copper sulfate, but today synthetic substances are used.

Moelleux
Describes sweet white wines, the sugar content of which may vary between 12 and 45 grams per liter, according to a 1984 EU directive.

Musky
A characteristic of wines made with the Muscatel grape as the base, especially during fermentation, when a smell reminiscent of musk is given off.

Must
Unfermented grape juice obtained by crushing or pressing.

NV
A contraction for nonvintage, used on Port, Champagne, or other wines; nonvintage wines can also be marketed as VSR (very special reserve).

Native yeast
A natural yeast attached to the skins of the grapes, sometimes solely used to start fermentation. If fermentation cannot be started by native, or indigenous, yeasts, then fabricated or synthetic yeasts are used.

Négociant	The person who buys wine from the grower or château to sell to wholesalers or foreign importers.
Négociant éleveur	The *négociant* who first buys wines from grower, then stores them in order to mature or blend them, or both. See **Elevage.**
Négociant manipulant	A term used for traders in Champagne who buy grapes at harvesttime for the preparation of their own Champagne. It is abbreviated to NM on the label.
New World	The European ex-colonies that began to produce wine in the fifteenth century. *See* **Old World.**
Noble rot	*See* **Rot, noble.**
Nouveau	Wine of the most recent **vintage,** which means that, after August 31 of the year following the vintage, wines can no longer claim this designation. Beaujolais Nouveau is the classic example. Now an increasing number of wine-producing regions always declare their vintage on the label; but in the regions of Oporto and Champagne, the vintage is still declared by the trade in the best years only.
Oidium	A disease of the vine caused by a microscopic mold that attacks the flowers, leaves, and grapes. The grapes dry out and a whitish dust covers the vine. The only remedy is sulfur treatment.
Old World	The countries of Europe and the Mediterranean basin that began to produce wine in the fourth century, as opposed to the **New World.** Old World winemakers, in principal, use more traditional winemaking techniques (blending grapes rather than producing single-variety wine, and insisting on smaller yields, for example) rather than modern science. They strive for individual style rather than a homogenous one and consider

terroir to be real and important. It might be suggested that the differences between the two are slowly fading, as some Old World winemakers are increasingly producing easy, noncommittal wines for export and to compete in this New World market, while some New World wine countries are embracing more traditional and less commercial styles. That said, the Old World still has time and experience on its side and, in my opinion, hold the ace card as far as possessing the indigenous grape varieties that are at home in their climates and soils.

Olive oil

Oil extracted from the flesh and stones of the olive. Like wine, the quality of the oil depends greatly on the type of olive, the harvest year, the climate, and the soil. Extra virgin is the highest quality, as it is unrefined from the first pressing (without aid of heat or chemicals) of the olives. This product is also known as cold-pressed extra virgin olive oil. The second pressing of the olives produces virgin olive oil, of lesser quality. The oil must be purified and filtered but it is not refined. The third type, pure olive oil, is a blend of extra-virgin and refined olive oil—the least-expensive and most common style.

Organoleptic

Smell, color, and taste make up what are called the organoleptic qualities perceived by the senses.

Overcropping

The practice of allowing vines to produce more fruit than they can ripen.

Oxidation

When oxygen in the air comes into direct contact with the wine, oxidation may cause changes in color and taste.

Oxidized

Sherry-like, madeirized, or nutty flavor caused by the action of oxygen on wine, due mainly to exposure to air, heat, and light.

Passerillage	The overripening of the grapes at harvest, causing drying out of the grape and higher sugar levels; this is how Vins de Paille, some Muscatels, and the sweet wines of the Jura are prepared. Not to be confused with the sweet wines obtained as a result of **noble rot.**
Pasteurization	To stabilize low-quality wines and get rid of any microorganisms, the wine can sometimes be pasteurized or heat-sterilized.
Perlant	Said of wines that are very slightly sparkling, but less so than semisparkling wines.
Pesto	Italian sauce made of basil, Parmesan, garlic, pine nuts, and olive oil.
pH	Measuring unit expressing potential hydrogen, or the concentration of H+ ions. For wines this means their degree of dryness (between 2.9 and 3.1 for the wines with the best bearing). The lower the pH, the safer the wine is from disease and oxidation, and therefore the greater its aging potential. *See also* **Acidity, real.**
Phylloxera	This plant louse, indigenous to the United States, attacks the vine at its roots. It was the cause of the destruction of the European vineyards between 1860 and 1880.
Polymerization	The process by which smaller molecules form and bind together to create larger ones. When wine ages, the phenolic molecules form and become larger tannin polymers, which become so large that they fall out of the wine and form sediment.
Pourriture noble	French for the *Botrytis cinerea* mold, literally "noble rot," *edelfäule* in German, which dehydrates grapes left late on the vine and concentrates their sweet juice.

Press wine

Press wine, or *vin de presse,* is obtained by pressing the more solid elements that are left over in the vat after the draining off of the free-run wines. Press wines are sometimes blended with the free-run wines at a later stage to obtain the best possible balance for the particular vintage.

Pressing

The operation whereby the grape juice is produced.

Primary aromas

Those smells in an unaged wine that actually emanate from the grape itself and are usually straightforward, fresh, and fruity. These change and become secondary (and tertiary when discussing Burgundies) after the wine has been oak aged. We then call the combination of aromas the wine's **bouquet.** A young wine cannot therefore have a bouquet.

Primeurs

These wines, designed to be drunk very young, enjoy this designation provided they are marketed from November 21 until January 31 of the following year. (Not to be confused with *en primeur.*)

QbA

Qualitätswein bestimmter Anbaugebiete; German wines that have been **chaptalized.**

QmP

Qualitätswein mit Prädikat, a designation is reserved for German wines of quality that have not been **chaptalized.**

Quinta

Portuguese equivalent of an estate or property. As with bodegas in Spain, Quinta wines may come from other properties than the one named.

Racking

The operation that separates the wine from the **lees;** it is called *soutirage* in French. This method aerates and clarifies wine by moving it from one container to another, leaving the lees and sediment behind in the first container.

Récoltant   A category of vinegrower in Champagne who makes
manipulant   his or her own Champagne (manipulates the grapes).

Reduction   The opposite, or complement, of **oxidation.** From
                       Jancis Robinson's *Oxford Companion to Wine,* page
                       781: "Wines, especially red wines held in the absence
                       of oxygen, may suffer from excess reduction; as a
                       result of the slow polymerisation of tannins and pig-
                       ments. A wine that is reduced tastes dirty and fre-
                       quently smells of reduced sulphur compounds such as
                       hydrogen sulphide and mercaptans." Aeration can
                       sometimes cure it.

Refrigeration   The physical process used to clarify wines by precipi-
                       tation of certain solid elements in them.

Remontage   For red wine, the operation of pumping the liquid up
                       from the bottom of the vat and spraying the cap. The
                       object is to achieve optimum contact between the liq-
                       uid and the sediment of skins, pips, and stalks floating
                       on the top.

Reserve   For wines and spirits, the term used for special *cuvées*
                       put aside for aging or future use. The term also refers
                       to a minimum aging period for certain spirits such as
                       calvados, cognac, and armagnac.

Residual sugar   The level of sugar that remains in wine after
(RS)   fermentation.

Riddling   A spectacular as well as basic operation in the *méthode*
                       champenoise by which deposits of dead yeasts and
                       mineral salts are collected round the cork so that they
                       can be removed. The French term is *remuage.*

Ripeness   A measurement of acid, **pH,** and sugar in the grapes;
                       the term is also important in conjunction with the
                       must, in order to extract more color and flavor.

Robe

Literally means "dress" in French and refers to the overall visual appearance of the wine, both in color and general appearance.

Rot, gray

Rot caused by the same mold as the **noble rot,** *Botrytis cinerea,* which affects grapes damaged by hail or grapeworm. High levels of humidity favor its development. Gray rot affects the quantity of the harvest, alters quality, and can lead to a disease in the wine called oxidasic casse.

Rot, noble

When conditions are favorable—with a dry, sunny end of autumn—grapes develop a beneficial form of decay thanks to the development of *Botrytis cinerea,* the celebrated mold that roasts the Sauternes grapes, producing a concentrated, different type of juice.

Rôti

Meaning "roasted," a characteristic of sweet wines with aromas of dried grapes resulting from noble rot.

Sec, Secco, Seco

"Dry" in French, Italian, and Portuguese or Spanish.

Selection by mass

Selection of grape varieties coming not from a single clone, but from a group of plants whose genetic structure is different.

Selection de grains nobles (SGN)

This expression, meaning "selection of noble grains," is used particularly in Alsace, but may also be used in other regions such as Sauternes, Barsac, Cadillac, Cérons, Loupiac, Ste-Croix-du-Mont, Monbazillac, Bonnezeaux, Quarts de Chaume, Coteaux du Layon, Coteaux de l'Aubance, Jurançon, and Graves Supérieures. It applies to wines made from late-picked grapes affected by noble rot or from *passerillés* grapes with a natural concentration of sugars.

Sorting

In the course of the harvest the sorting, or *triage,* is the stage during which green or rotten grapes are removed. *Sorting* is also the term used for the successive pickings used in the harvest of *passerillés* grapes or grapes affected by **noble rot.** Also can apply to the process of sorting the healthy grapes from the unhealthy, after harvesting, on the sorting tables.

Sour A fungus *(Mycoderma aceti)* that causes wine to change into vinegar when in contact with air. It develops particularly in inadequately filled vats, giving the wine a sour taste and an extremely unpleasant smell.

Spätlese Late-harvested German wines.

Sparkling There are several ways of making a sparkling wine: *méthode champenoise;* what is known as the rural method (for instance, Gaillac, Die), when effervescence is the result of a secondary fermentation; and the Charmat or *cuve close* method. Effervescence may also be produced by adding carbon dioxide.

Stemming The process of separating the grapes from the stalks. The stalks contain oils and **tannins** that tend to make the wine bitter and harsh. There is sometimes a need for this process when the grapes are too soft or lack acidity and structure; the stems can provide some of the body and firmness that are missing.

Stemmy An unpleasant aroma and taste of wine fermented with an excess use of grape and stems.

Still wines The opposite of **sparkling** wines, the term also describes wines that are used as a base in the making of sparkling and semisparkling wines.

Sulfur dioxide Winemakers have always used sulfur because of its numerous qualities: It checks premature fermentation in the harvested grapes; destroys undesirable yeasts; eliminates microbes and bacteria; protects **oxidation;** acts as a dissolving agent; and is a precious ally for sweet white wines inclined to referment in the bottle. Sulfur dioxide is now used either in gaseous form or diluted in water at 5 percent or 18 percent. Too much sulfur dioxide can produce a taste of rotten eggs and induce headaches.

Sur lie   Allowing the wine to be aged in contact with the **lees,** the expired yeast cells from fermentation. Usually considered to give the wine more taste and extracts.

Taille   The process of pruning the vines' branches in winter into the shape that will allow them to bear the most fruit, bearing in mind the soil, climate, and grape variety. In Champagne, it indicates the part of the **must** that is drawn off by pressing after the **cuvée.** There is a distinction between the first and second taille.

Tannin   In English we tend to speak of tannin in the singular; this is inaccurate, as there are different types of tannin, all derived from vegetable substances such as nuts, wood, bark, berries, and, of course, grapes. The stalks, skins, and pips contain tannins, which are released during the fermentation process and the pressing, giving the wine its specific character and contributing to its capacity for aging. Storing the wine in new wood allows additional tannin contained in the fibers of the wood to be absorbed by the wine.

Tart   A rough and harsh sensation in the mouth caused by excess **tannins.** These are caused by either a rustic grape variety or excessive fermentation.

Terroir   An all-encompassing French term referring to the particular characteristics of a specific piece of vineyard land, including but not limited to the sum total of soil, exposure, drainage, climate, trellising, and grape variety. More poetically, it is the unique and magic trilogy of climate, grape, and soil.

Thermo-regulation   The process of controlling the temperature of vats during fermentation.

Thinning   A few days before the harvest, it is often helpful to remove the leaves covering the grapes to make the grapes riper and more healthy.

Ullage   The vacant area in a bottle or cask between the wine and the cork or roof of the cask. Bottle ullage increases with time, as the wine breathes through the cork. Always look out for excessive ullage when buying an older wine.

Varietal   A varietal, or *vin de cépage,* is a wine made from a single grape variety. In France the wine must contain 100 percent of the same variety; in some other countries small proportions of other varieties are allowed, and in others there is no relevant regulation. This is also said of wine which has the pronounced aroma and flavor of a grape variety and is the general term for wines labeled with names of grape varieties.

Vat room   The vat room, or *cuvier,* is where the vats or **cuves** are kept.

Vendanges tardives (VT)   This means "late harvesting," which is done to procure overripe grapes for sweet wines.

Viniculture   The science or study of grape production for wine and of the making of wine.

Vins sur lattes   Wines that have been made into Champagne and are stockpiled on their **lees** prior to **riddling.**

Vintage   Originally meaning "the grape harvest," because there is only one per year, the term has come to refer to the wine made from the harvest of a particular year. Each vintage acquires its specific nature from a combination of climatic factors that will determine the wine's quality and potential for aging.

The differences in quality from one year to another are such that most *négociants* blend wines from different vintages to create a better-balanced product; but the outstanding vintages deserve to stand on their own, so they are kept as single harvest stock to be made available as vintages. In the past such vintages were very rare, and wines were sold as NV (nonvintage) or VSR (very special reserve).

Viticulture   The cultivation, science, and study of grapes.

SUGGESTED READING

These are some of my favorite food and wine reference books from my personal library. I am always looking out for good material, so please do not hesitate to contact me via the publisher with anything you have come across that you find indispensable. For this book, I referred to these, as well as ten years of my tasting notes, excerpts from my previously published articles in *Vintage* magazine, my first book *The Wine Collector's Handbook,* countless international and regional cookbooks, my husband's gardening encyclopedias, magazine articles clipped throughout the years, winery brochures, and saved menus from hundreds of wine dinners enjoyed across Europe and other delicious corners of the globe.

Anderson, Burton. *Wines of Italy.* London: Italian Trade Centre, 1992.

Ayrton, Elisabeth. *The Cookery of England.* London: Purnell Books Services Limited, 1975.

Gribourg, G., and C. Sarfati. *La Dégustation* (Edisud, Université du Vin, Suze-la-Rousse, 1989).

Johnson-Bell, Linda. *The Wine Collector's Handbook.* New York: The Lyons Press, 1997.

Montagné, Prosper. *Larousse Gastronomique.* Translated by Paul Hamlyn. London, 1961.

Peynaud, Emile. *Knowing and Making Wine.* Translated by Alan Spencer. Chichester, Sussex: John Wiley and Sons, 1981.

Robinson, Jancis. *Guide to Wine Grapes.* Oxford University Press, 1996.

Robinson, Jancis, ed. *The Oxford Companion to Wine.* Oxford University Press, 1994.

Wilson, James E. *Terroir.* London: Mitchell Beazley, Reed Books, 1998.

INDEX

Note: Entries in the Food to Wine and Wine to Food cross references do not appear in the following index. Only text portions of the book have been indexed. *Italic* page numbers indicate charts within the text.